SHAKESPEARE

ROMEO
AND JULIET

NOTES

COLES EDITORIAL BOARD

ABOUT COLES NOTES

COLES NOTES have been an indispensible aid to students on five continents since 1948.

COLES NOTES are available for a wide range of individual literary works. Clear, concise explanations and insights are provided along with interesting interpretations and evaluations.

Proper use of COLES NOTES will allow the student to pay greater attention to lectures and spend less time taking notes. This will result in a broader understanding of the work being studied and will free the student for increased participation in discussions.

COLES NOTES are an invaluable aid for review and exam preparation as well as an invitation to explore different interpretive paths.

COLES NOTES are written by experts in their fields. It should be noted that any literary judgement expressed herein is just that — the judgement of one school of thought. Interpretations that diverge from, or totally disagree with any criticism may be equally valid.

COLES NOTES are designed to supplement the text and are not intended as a substitute for reading the text itself. Use of the NOTES will serve not only to clarify the work being studied, but should enhance the reader's enjoyment of the topic.

ISBN 0-7740-3228-6

© COPYRIGHT 1988 AND PUBLISHED BY
COLES PUBLISHING COMPANY LIMITED
TORONTO—CANADA
PRINTED IN CANADA

Manufactured by Webcom Limited
Cover finish: Webcom's Exclusive **Duracoat**

CONTENTS

Structure

Characters

Meaning

Style

WILLIAM SHAKESPEARE: LIFE AND WORKS
Biographical Sketch

The Early Years

Despite the scholarship it has generated, our knowledge of Shakespeare's life is sketchy, filled with more questions than answers, even after we discard the misinformation accumulated over the years. He was baptized on April 26, 1564, in Holy Trinity Church, Stratford-on-Avon. As it was customary to baptize children a few days after birth, he was probably born on April 23. The monument erected in Stratford states that he died on April 23, 1616, in his fifty-third year.

William was the third child of John Shakespeare, who came to Stratford from Snitterfield before 1532 as a "whyttawer" (tanner) and glover, and Mary Arden, daughter of a wealthy "gentleman of worship" from Wilmecote. They married around 1557. Since John Shakespeare owned one house on Greenhill Street and two on Henley Street, we cannot be certain where William was born, though the Henley Street shrine draws many tourists each year. William's two older sisters died in infancy, but three brothers and two other sisters survived at least into childhood.

Shakespeare's father was well-to-do, dealing in farm products and wool, and owning considerable property in Stratford. After holding a series of minor municipal offices he was elected alderman in 1565, high bailiff (roughly similar to the mayor of today) in 1568, and chief alderman in 1571. There are no records of young Will Shakespeare's education (though there are many unfounded legends), but he probably attended the town school maintained by the burgesses, which prepared its students for the universities. Ben Jonson's line about Shakespeare's having "small *Latine*, and lesse *Greeke*" refers not to his education but to his lack of indebtedness to the classical writers and dramatists.

On November 27, 1582, a licence to marry was issued to "Willelmum Shaxpere *et* Annam Whateley *de* Temple Grafton." On the next day a marriage bond for "Willm Shagspere" and "Anne Hathwey of Stratford" was signed by Fulk Sandells and John Richardson, farmers of Stratford. This bond stated that there was no "lawful let or impediment by reason of any precontract, consanguinity, affinity, or by any other lawful means whatsoever"; thus "William and Anne (were) to be married together with once asking of the banns of matrimony." The problem of Anne Whateley has led many researchers to argue all kinds of improbabilities, such as the existence of two different Shakespeares and the forging of documents to conceal Shakespeare's true identity. The actual explanation seems to be simple: the clerk who

1

made the marriage licence entry apparently copied the name "Whateley" from a preceding entry, as a glance at the full sheet suggests. (Incidentally, Nicholas Rowe in his life of Shakespeare, published in 1709, well before the discovery of these marriage records, gave Anne's name as Hathaway.) The problems of marriage with Anne Hathaway — he was eighteen and she was twenty-six — and of the bond have caused similar consternation. Why did these two marry when there was such a discrepancy of age? Why only one saying of the banns (rather than the usual three)? Why the emphasis on a possible legal problem? The answer here is not simple or definite, but the birth of a daughter Susanna, baptized at Holy Trinity on May 26, 1583, seems to explain the odd circumstances. It should be recognized, however, that an engagement to marry was considered legally binding in those days (we still have breach-of-promise suits today) and that premarital relations were not unusual or frowned upon when an engagement had taken place. The circumstances already mentioned, Shakespeare's ensuing activities, and his will bequeathing to Anne "my second best bed with the furniture" have suggested to some that their marriage was not entirely happy. Their other children, the twins Hamnet and Judith, were christened on February 2, 1585.

Theatrical Life

Shakespeare's years before and immediately after the time of his marriage are not charted, but rumor has him as an apprentice to a master butcher or as a country teacher or an actor with some provincial company. He is supposed to have run away from whatever he was doing for livelihood and to have gone to London, where he soon joined a theatrical group. At this time there were only two professional houses established in London, The Theatre (opened in 1576) and The Curtain (opened in 1577). His first connection with the theater was reputedly as holder of horses; that is, one of the stage crew, but a most inferior assignment. Thereafter he became an actor (perhaps at this time he met Ben Johnson), a writer, and a director. Such experience had its mark in the theatricality of his plays. We do know that he was established in London by 1592, when Robert Greene lamented in *A Groatsworth of Wit* (September, 1592) that professional actors had gained priority in the theater over university-trained writers like himself: "There is an upstart Crow, beautified with our feathers, that with his *Tygers hart wrapt in a Players hyde,* supposes he is as well able to bombast out a lanke verse as the best of you: and beeing an absolute *Iohannes fac totum* (Jack-of-all-trades), is in his owne conceit the onely Shake-scene in a countrey." An apology for Greene's ill-humored statement by Henry Chettle, the editor of the pamphlet, appeared around December 1592 in *Kind-Hart's Dream.*

Family Affairs

To return to the known details of his family life, Shakespeare's son Hamnet was buried at Stratford on August 11, 1596; his father was given a coat of arms on October 20, 1596; and Will purchased New Place (a refurbished tourist attraction today) on May 4, 1597. The London playwright obviously had not severed connections with his birthplace, and he was reflecting his new affluence by being known as William Shakespeare of Stratford-upon-Avon, in the County of Warwick, Gentleman. His father was buried in Stratford on September 8, 1601; his mother, on September 9, 1608. His daughter Susanna married Dr. John Hall on June 5, 1607, and they had a child named Elizabeth. His other daughter, Judith, married Thomas Quiney on February 10, 1616, without special licence, during Lent and was thus excommunicated. Shakespeare revised his will on March 25, 1616, and was buried on April 25, 1616 (according to the parish register). A monument by Gerard Janssen was erected in the Holy Trinity chancel in 1623 but many, like Milton several years later, protested:

> What needs my *Shakespeare* for his honour'd Bones,
> The labour of an age in piled Stone, . . .
> Thou in our wonder and astonishment
> Hast built thy self a live-long Monument.

Shakespeare's Writings

Order of Appearance

Dating of Shakespeare's early plays, while based on inconclusive evidence, has tended to hover around the early 1590s. Almost certainly, it is his chronicles of Henry the Sixth that Philip Henslowe, an important theatrical manager of the day, referred to in his diary as being performed during March-May, 1592. An allusion to these plays also occurs in Thomas Nashe's *Piers Penniless His Supplication to the Devil* (August, 1592).

The first published work to come from Shakespeare's hand was *Venus and Adonis* (1593), a long poem, dedicated to Henry Wriothesley, Earl of Southampton. A year later *The Rape of Lucrece* appeared, also dedicated to Southampton. Perhaps poetry was pursued during these years because the London theaters were closed as a result of an outbreak of plague. The *Sonnets*, published in 1609, may owe something to Southampton, who had become Shakespeare's patron. Perhaps some were written as early as the first few years of the 1590's. They were mentioned (along with a number of plays) in 1598 by Francis Meres in his *Palladis Tamia*, and sonnets 138 and 144 were printed without authority by William Jaggard in *The Passionate Pilgrim* (1599).

There is a record of a performance of *A Comedy of Errors* at Gray's Inn (one of the law colleges) on December 28, 1594, and,

3

during early 1595, Shakespeare was paid, along with the famous actors Richard Burbage and William Kempe, for performances before the Queen by the Lord Chamberlain's Men, a theatrical company formed the year before. The company founded the Globe Theatre in 1599 and became the King's Men when James ascended the throne. Records show frequent payments to the company through its general manager John Heminge. From 1595 through 1614 there are numerous references to real estate transactions and other legal matters, to many performances, and to various publications connected with Shakespeare.

Order of Publication

The first plays to be printed were *Titus Andronicus* around February, 1594, and the garbled versions of *Henry VI*, Parts II and III in 1594. Thereafter *Richard III* appeared in 1597 and 1598; *Richard II*, in 1597 and twice in 1958; *Romeo and Juliet*, in 1597 (a pirated edition) and 1599, and many others. Some of the plays appear in individual editions, with or without Shakespeare's name on the title page, but eighteen are known only from their appearance in the first collected volume (the so-called First Folio) of 1623. The editors were Heminge and Henry Condell, another member of Shakespeare's company. *Pericles* was omitted from the First Folio although it had appeared in 1609, 1611, and 1619; it was added to the Third Folio in 1664.

There was reluctance to publish plays at this time for various reasons; many plays were carelessly written for fast production; collaboration was frequent; plays were not really considered *reading* matter; they were sometimes circulated in manuscript; and the theatrical company, not the author, owned the rights. Those plays given individual publication appeared in a quarto, so named from the size of the page. A single sheet of paper was folded twice to make four leaves (thus *quarto*) or eight pages; these four leaves constitute one signature (one section of a bound book). A page measures about 6-3/4 in. × 8-1/2 in. On the other hand, a folio sheet is folded once to make two leaves or four pages; three sheets, or twelve pages, constitute a signature. The page is approximately 8-1/2 in. × 13-3/4 in.

Authorized publication occurred when a company disbanded, when money was needed but rights were to be retained, when a play failed or ran into licensing difficulties (thus, hopefully, the printed work would justify the play against the criticism), or when a play had been pirated. Authorized editions are called good quartos. Piratical publication might occur when the manuscript of a play had circulated privately, when a member of a company desired money for himself, or when a stenographer or memorizer took the play down in the theater (such a version was recognizable by inclusion of stage directions derived from an eyewitness, by garbled sections, etc.). Pirated editions

4

are called bad quartos; there are at least five bad quartos of Shakespeare's plays.

Authenticity of Works

Usually thirty-seven plays are printed in modern collections of Shakespeare's works but some recent scholars have urged the addition of two more: *Edward III* and *Two Noble Kinsmen*. At times, six of the generally-accepted plays have been questioned: *Henry I,* Parts I, II and III, *Timon of Athens, Pericles* and *Henry VIII*. The first four are usually accepted today (one hopes all question concerning *Timon* has finally ended), but if Shakespeare did not write these plays in their entirety, he certainly wrote parts of them. Of course, collaboration in those days was common. Aside from the two long narrative poems already mentioned and the sonnets (Nos. 1-152, but not Nos. 153-154), Shakespeare's poetic output is uncertain. *The Passionate Pilgrim* (1599) contains only five authenticated poems (two sonnets and three verses from *Love's Labour's Lost*); *The Phoenix and the Turtle* (1601) may be his, but the authenticity of *A Lover's Complaint* (appended to the sonnets) is highly questionable.

Who Was Shakespeare?

At this point we might mention a problem that has plagued Shakespeare study for over a century: who was Shakespeare? Those who would like to make the author of the plays someone else — Francis Bacon or the Earl of Oxford or even Christopher Marlowe (dead long before most of the plays were written) — have used the lack of information of Shakespeare's early years and the confusion in the evidence we have been examining to advance their candidate. But the major arguments against Shakespeare show the source of these speculators' disbelief to be in classconscious snobbery and perhaps in a perverse adherence to minority opinion. The most common argument is that no one of Shakespeare's background, lack of education, and lack of aristocratic experience could know all that the author knew. But study will reveal that such information was readily available in various popular sources, that some of it lies in the literary sources used for the play, and that Shakespeare was probably not totally lacking in education or in social decorum. The more significant question of style and tone is not dealt with — nor could it successfully be raised. Bacon, for example, no matter how much we admire his mind and his writings, exhibits a writing style diametrically opposite to Shakespeare's, a style most unpoetic and often flat. The student would be wise not to waste time rehashing these unfounded theories. No such question was raised in the seventeenth or eighteenth centuries, and no serious student of the plays today doubts that Shakespeare *was* Shakespeare.

Shakespeare's Plays

Exact dates for Shakespeare's plays remain a source of debate among scholars. The following serve only as a general frame of reference.

COMEDIES	TRAGEDIES	HISTORIES
1591		Henry VI, Part I
1592 Comedy of Errors		Henry VI, Part II
1592 Two Gentlemen of Verona		Henry VI, Part III
1593 Love's Labour's Lost	Titus Andronicus	Richard III
1594		King John
1595 Midsummer Night's Dream	Romeo and Juliet	Richard II
1596 Merchant of Venice		
1596 Taming of the Shrew		
1597		Henry IV, Part I
1598 Much Ado About Nothing		Henry IV, Part II
1599 As You Like It	Julius Caesar	
1599 Merry Wives of Windsor		Henry V
1601 Twelfth Night	Hamlet	
1602 Troilus and Cressida		
1602 All's Well That Ends Well		
1604 Measure for Measure	Othello	
1605	King Lear	
1606	Macbeth	
1607	Timon of Athens	
1607	Antony and Cleopatra	
1608 Pericles		
1609	Coriolanus	
1610 Cymbeline		
1611 Winter's Tale		
1611 Tempest		
1613		Henry VIII

Shakespeare's England

The world of Elizabethan and Jacobean England was a world of growth and change. The great increase in the middle class, and in the population as a whole, demanded a new economy and means of livelihood, a new instrument of government (one recognizing "rights" and changed class structure), a new social code and a broad base of entertainment. The invention of printing a century before had contributed to that broader base, but it was the theater that supplied the more immediate needs of the greatest numbers. The theater grew and along with it came less-educated, more money-conscious writers, who gave the people what they wanted: entertainment. But Shakespeare, having passed through a brief period of hack writing, proceeded to set down important ideas in memorable language throughout most of his career. His plays, particularly the later ones, have been analyzed by recent critics in terms of literary quality through their metaphor, verse-line, relationships with psychology and myth, and elaborate structure. Yet Shakespeare was a man of the stage, and the plays were written to be performed. Only this will fully account for the humor of a deadly serious play like *Hamlet* or the spectacle of a *Coriolanus*.

Life in London

During Shakespeare's early years there, London was a walled city of about 200,000, with seven gates providing access to the city from the east, north and west. It was geographically small and crisscrossed by narrow little streets and lanes. The various wards each had a parish church that dominated the life of the close-knit community. To the south and outside were slums and the haunts of criminal types, and farther out were the agricultural lands and huge estates. As the population increased and the central area declined, the fashionable people of the city moved toward the west, where the palace of Westminster lay. Houses were generally rented out floor by floor and sometimes room by room. Slums were common within the city, too, though close to pleasant enough streets and squares. "Merrie Olde England" was not really clean, nor were its people, for in those days that were no sewers or drains except the gutter in the middle of the street, into which garbage would be emptied to be floated off by the rain. Plague was particularly ravaging in 1592, 1593-94 (when the theaters were closed to avoid contamination) and 1603. Medical knowledge, of course, was slight; ills were "cured" by amputation, leeching and blood-letting. The city was (and still is) dominated by St. Paul's Cathedral, around which booksellers clustered on Paternoster Row.

Religious Atmosphere

Of great significance for the times was religion. Under Elizabeth, a state church had developed; it was Protestant in nature and was called Anglican (or today, Episcopalian). It had arisen from Henry VIII's break with the Pope and from a compromise with the Roman Catholics who had gained power under Mary Tudor.

The Church of England was headed by the Archbishop of Canterbury who was to be an increasingly important figure in the early part of the seventeenth century. There were also many schismatic groups, which generally desired further departures from Roman Catholicism. Calvinists were perhaps the most numerous and important of the Protestant groups. The Puritans, who were Calvinist, wanted to "purify" the church of ritual and certain ideas, but during the 1590s they were labeled as extremists in dress and conduct.

Political Milieu

During Shakespeare's lifetime there were two monarchs: Elizabeth, 1558-1603, and James I, 1603-1625. Elizabeth was the daughter of Henry VIII and Anne Boleyn, his second wife, who was executed in 1536. After Henry's death, his son by his third wife, Jane Seymour (who died in 1537), reigned as Edward VI. He was followed by Mary Tudor, daughter of Henry's first wife, Catherine of Aragon. Mary was a Roman Catholic, who tried to put down religious dissension by persecution of both Protestants and Catholics. Nor did her marriage to Philip II of Spain endear her to the people.

Elizabeth's reign was troubled by many offers of marriage, particularly from Spanish and French nobles — all Roman Catholic — and by the people's concern for an heir to the throne. English suitors generally cancelled one another out by intrigue or aggressiveness. One of the most prominent was the Earl of Essex, Robert Devereux, who fell in and out of favor; he apparently attempted to take over the reins of control, only to be captured, imprisoned and executed in February, 1601. One claimant to the throne was Mary of Scotland, a Roman Catholic and widow of Francis II of France. She was the second cousin of Elizabeth, tracing her claim through her grandmother, who was Henry VIII's sister. Finally, settlement came with Elizabeth's acceptance of Mary's son as heir apparent, though Mary was to be captured, tried and executed for treason in 1587. Mary had abdicated the throne of Scotland in 1567 in favor of her son, James VI. His ascent to the throne of England in 1603 as James I joined the two kingdoms for the first time, although Scotland during the seventeenth century often acted independently of England.

Contemporary Events

Political and religious problems were intermingled in the celebrated Gunpowder Plot. Angry over fines that were levied upon those not attending Church of England services — primarily Roman Catholics — and offended by difficulties over papal envoys, a group of Catholics plotted to blow up Parliament, and James with it, at its first session on November 5, 1605. A cache of gunpowder was stored in the cellar, guarded by various conspirators, among them Guy Fawkes. The plot was discovered before it could be carried out and Fawkes, on duty at the time, was arrested. The execution of the plotters and the triumph of the anti-Papists led in succeeding years to celebrations in the streets and the hanging of Fawkes in effigy.

Among the most noteworthy public events during these times were the wars with the Spanish, which included the defeat of the Spanish Armada in 1588, the battle in the Lowlands in 1590-1594, the expedition to Cadiz under Essex in 1596 and the expedition to the Azores (the Islands Expedition), also under Essex, in 1597. With trading companies specially set up for colonization and exploitation, travel excited the imagination of the people: here was a new way of life, here were new customs brought back by the sailors and merchants, here was a new world to explore.

In all, the years from around 1590 to 1601 were trying ones for English people, relieved only by the news from abroad, the new affluence and the hope for the future under James. Writers of this period frequently reflect, however, the disillusionment and sadness of those difficult times.

The Elizabethan Theater

Appearance

The Elizabethan playhouse developed from the medieval inn with its rooms grouped around a courtyard into which a stage was built. This pattern was used in The Theatre, built by James Burbage in 1576: a square frame building (later round or octagonal) with a square yard, three tiers of galleries, each jutting out over the one below, and a stage extending into the middle of the yard, where people stood or sat on improvised seats. There was no cover over the yard or stage and lighting was therefore natural. Performances were held in the afternoon.

Other theaters were constructed over the years: The Curtain in 1577, The Rose in 1587 (on Bankside), The Swan in 1595 (also Bankside) and Shakespeare's playhouse, The Globe, in 1599 (not far from The Rose). There is still some question about the exact dimensions of this house, but it seems to have been octagonal, each side measuring about 36 feet, with an over-all diameter of 84 feet. It was about 33 feet to the eaves, and the yard was 56 feet in diameter. Three sides were used for backstage and to serve the needs of the players. The stage jutted out into the audience and there was no curtain. The spectators often became part of the action. Obviously, the actors' asides and soliloquies were effective under these conditions.

There was no real scenery and there were only a few major props. Thus the lines of the play had to reveal locations and movement, changes in time or place, etc. In this way, too, it was easier to establish a nonrealistic setting, for all settings were created in words. On either side of the stage were doors, within the flooring were trapdoors (for entrances of ghosts, etc.), and behind the main stage was the inner stage or recess. Here, indoor scenes (such as a court or a bedchamber) were played, and some props could be used because the inner stage was usually concealed by a curtain when not in use. It might also have served to hide someone behind the ever-present arras (hanging tapestry), like Polonius in *Hamlet*. The "chamber" was on the second level, with windows and a balcony. On the third level was another chamber, primarily for musicians.

Actors

An acting company such as the Lord Chamberlain's Men was a fellowship of ten to fifteen sharers with some ten to twelve extras, three or four boys (often to play women's roles) who might become full sharers, and stagehands. There were rival companies, each with its leading dramatist and leading tragic actor and clown. The Lord Admiral's Men, organized in 1594, boasted Ben Jonson and the tragedian Edward Alleyn. Some of the rivalry of this War of the Theaters is reflected in the speeches of Hamlet, who comments on the ascendancy and unwarranted popularity of the children's companies (like the Children of Blackfriars) in the late 1590s.

The company dramatist, of course, had to think in terms of the members of his company as he wrote his play. He had to make use of the physical features and peculiar talents of the actors, making sure, besides, that there was a role for each member. The fact that women's parts were taken by boys imposed obvious limitations on the range of action. Accordingly, we often find women characters impersonating men. For example, Robert Goffe played Portia in *The Merchant of Venice*, and Portia impersonates a male lawyer in the important trial scene. Goffe also played Juliet, and Anne in *Richard III*, and Oberon in *A Midsummer Night's Dream*. The influence of an actor on the playwright can be seen, on the one hand, by noting the "humor" characters portrayed so competently by Thomas Pope, who was a choleric Mercutio in *Romeo*, a melancholic Jaques in *As You Like It*, and a sanguinary Falstaff in *Henry IV*, Part I; and by comparing, on the other hand, the clown Bottom in *A Midsummer Night's Dream*, played in a frolicsome manner by William Kempe, with the clown Feste in *Twelfth Night*, sung and danced by Robert Armin. Obviously, too, if a certain kind of character was not available within the company, then that kind of character could not be written into the play. The approach was decidedly different from ours today, where the play almost always comes first and the casting of roles second. The plays were performed in a repertory system, with a different play each afternoon. The average life of a play was about ten performances.

History of the Drama

English drama goes back to native forms developed from playlets presented at Church holidays. Mystery plays dealt with biblical stories such as the Nativity or the Passion, and miracle plays usually depicted the lives of saints. The merchant and craft guilds that came to own and produce the cycles of plays were the forerunners of the theatrical companies of Shakespeare's time. The kind of production these cycles received, either as moving pageants in the streets or as staged shows in a churchyard, influenced the late sixteenth-century production of a secular play: there was an intimacy with the audience and there was a great reliance on words rather than setting and props. Similar involvement with the stage action is experienced by audiences of the arena theater of today.

The morality play, the next form to develop, was an allegory of the

10

spiritual conflict between good and evil in the soul of man. The *dramatis personae* were abstract virtues and vices, with at least one man representing Mankind (or Everyman, as the most popular of these plays was titled). Some modern critics see *Othello* as a kind of morality play in which the soul of Othello is vied for by the aggressively evil Iago (as a kind of Satanic figure) and passively good Desdemona (as a personification of Christian faith in all men). The Tudor interlude — a short, witty, visual play — may have influenced the subplot of the Elizabethan play with its low-life and jesting and visual tricks. In mid-sixteenth century appeared the earliest known English comedies, Nicholas Udall's *Ralph Roister Doister* and *Gammer Gurton's Needle* (of uncertain authorship). Both show the influence of the Roman comic playwright Plautus. Shakespeare's *Comedy of Errors*, performed in the 1590's, was an adaptation of Plautus' *Menaechmi*, both plays featuring twins and an involved story of confused identities. The influence of the Roman tragedian Seneca can be traced from Thomas Norton and Thomas Sackville in *Gorboduc* to *Hamlet*. Senecan tragedy is a tragedy of revenge, characterized by many deaths, much blood-letting, ghosts, feigned madness and the motif of a death for a death.

Shakespeare's Artistry

Plots

Generally, a Shakespearean play has two plots: a main plot and a subplot. The subplot reflects the main plot and is often concerned with inferior characters. Two contrasting examples will suffice: Lear and his daughters furnish the characters for the main plot of filial love and ingratitude. Gloucester and his sons enact the same theme in the subplot. Lear and Gloucester both learn that outward signs of love may be false. In *A Midsummer Night's Dream*, the town workmen (Quince, Bottom *et al.*) put on a tragic play in such a hilarious way that it turns the subject of the play — love so strong that the hero will kill himself if his loved one dies first — into farce, but this in the main plot is the "serious" plight of the four mixed-up lovers. In both examples Shakespeare has reinforced his points by subplots dealing with the same subject as the main plot.

Sources

The plots of the Elizabethan plays were usually adapted from other sources. Originality was not the sought quality; a kind of variation on a theme was. It was felt that one could better evaluate the playwright's worth by seeing what he did with a familiar tale. What he stressed, how he stressed it, how he restructured the familiar elements — these were the important matters. Shakespeare closely followed Sir Thomas North's popular translation of Plutarch's *Life of Marcus*

Antonius, for example, in writing *Antony and Cleopatra.* He modified Robert Greene's *Pandosto* and combined it with the Pygmalion myth in *The Winter's Tale,* while drawing the character of Autolycus from certain pamphlets written by Greene. The only plays for which sources have not been clearly determined are *Love's Labour's Lost* (probably based on contemporary events) and *The Tempest* (possibly based on some shipwreck account from travelers to the New World).

Verse and Prose

There is a mixture of verse and prose in the plays, partially because plays fully in verse were out of fashion. Greater variety could thus be achieved and character or atmosphere could be more precisely delineated. Elevated passages, philosophically significant ideas, speeches by men of high rank are in verse, but comic and light parts, speeches including dialect or broken English, and scenes that move more rapidly or simply give mundane information are in prose. The poetry is almost always blank verse (iambic pentameter lines without rhyme). Rhyme is used, however (particularly the couplet), to mark the close of scenes or an important action. Rhyme also serves as a cue for the entrance of another actor or some off-stage business, to point to a change of mood or thought, as a forceful opening after a passage of prose, to convey excitement or passion or sentimentality and to distinguish characters.

Shakespeare's plays may be divided into three general categories, though some plays are not readily classified and further subdivisions may be suggested within a category.

The History Play

The history play, or chronicle, may tend to tragedy, like *Richard II,* or to comedy, like *Henry IV,* Part I. It is a chronicle of some royal personage, often altered for dramatic purposes, even to the point of falsifying the facts. Its popularity may have resulted from the rising of nationalism of the English, nurtured by their successes against the Spanish, their developing trade and colonization, and their rising prestige as a world power. The chronicle was considered a political guide, like the popular *Mirror for Magistrates,* a collection of writings showing what happens when an important leader falls through some error in his ways, his thinking or his personality. Thus the history play counsells the right path by negative, if not positive, means. Accordingly, it is difficult to call *Richard II* a tragedy, since Richard was wrong and his wrongness harmed his people. The political philosophy of Shakespeare's day seemed to favor the view that all usurpation was bad and should be corrected, but not by further usurpation. When that original usurpation had been established, through an heir's ascension to the throne, it was to be accepted. Then any rebellion against the "true" king would be a rebellion against God.

12

Tragedy

Tragedy, in simple terms, means that the protagonist dies. Certain concepts drawn from Aristotle's *Poetics* require a tragic hero of high standing, who must oppose some conflicting force, either external or internal. The tragic hero should be dominated by a *hamartia* (a so-called tragic flaw, but really an *excess* of some character trait, e.g., pride, or *hubris*), and it is this *hamartia* that leads to his downfall and, because of his status, to the downfall of others. The action presented in the tragedy must be recognizable to the audience as real. Through seeing it enacted, the audience has its passion (emotions) raised, and the conclusion of the action thus brings release from that passion (*catharsis*). A more meaningful way of looking at tragedy in the Elizabethan theater, however, is to see it as that which occurs when essential good (like Hamlet) is wasted (through disaster or death) in the process of driving out evil (such as Claudius represents).

Comedy

Comedy in simple terms means that the play ends happily for the protagonists. Sometimes the comedy depends on exaggerations of man's eccentricities — comedy of humors; sometimes the comedy is romantic and far-fetched. The romantic comedy was usually based on a mix-up in events or confused identity of characters, particularly by disguise. It moves towards tragedy in that an important person might die and the mix-up might never be unraveled; but in the nick of time something happens or someone appears (sometimes illogically or unexpectedly) and saves the day. It reflects the structure of myth by moving from happiness to despair to resurrection. *The Winter's Tale* is a perfect example of this, for the happiness of the first part is banished with Hermione's exile and Perdita's abandonment. Tragedy is near when the lost baby, Perdita, cannot be found and Hermione is presumed dead. But Perdita reappears, as does Hermione, a statue that suddenly comes to life. Lost identities are established and confusions disappear but the mythic-comic nature of the play is seen in the reuniting of the mother, Hermione, a kind of Ceres, with her daughter, Perdita, a kind of Proserpina. Spring returns, summer will bring the harvest, and the winter of the tale is left behind — for a little while.

What is it, then, that makes Shakespeare's art so great? Perhaps we see in it a whole spectrum of humanity, treated impersonally, but with kindness and understanding. We seldom meet in Shakespeare a weeping philosopher: he may criticize, but he criticizes both sides. After he has done so, he gives the impression of saying, Well, that's the way life is; people will always be like that — don't get upset about it. This is probably the key to the Duke's behavior in *Measure for Measure* — a most unbitter comedy despite former labels. Only in *Hamlet* does Shakespeare not seem to fit this statement; it is the one play that Shakespeare, the person, enters.

As we grow older and our range of experience widens, so, too, does Shakespeare's range seem to expand. Perhaps this lies in the ambiguities of his own materials, which allow for numerous individual readings. We meet our own experiences — and they are ours alone, we think — expressed in phrases that we thought our own or our own discovery. What makes Shakespeare's art so great, then, is his ability to say so much to so many people in such memorable language: he is himself "the show and gaze o' the time."

ROMEO AND JULIET

Plot Summary

A sonnet prologue to the play explains that two households in Verona, the Capulets and Montagues, are engaged in a blood feud, the daughter of the Capulets, Juliet, and the son of the Montagues, Romeo, will fall in love and meet their deaths.

The play itself begins with an exchange between two servants of the Capulets, Sampson and Gregory, in which they entertain the audience with puns and jokes. Two servants of the Montagues enter; the Capulet servants seeing Benvolio in the distance begin a quarrel. Benvolio comes on stage and attempts to beat down their swords. At this instant Tybalt, a fiery kinsman of Capulet, enters, and the battle becomes serious. Prince Escalus arrives, stops the fighting, and orders the two families to keep the peace, ironically on penalty of death. After the fray Benvolio remains on stage with the Montagues; they discuss Romeo, who is suffering from love. Benvolio agrees to discover for the father the cause of Romeo's melancholy, and when Romeo enters they begin an elaborate word game the subject of which is Romeo's romance and the pain he is suffering because of his mistress, Rosaline.

The scene changes to a discussion between Old Capulet and Paris. Paris is suing for the hand of Juliet. Capulet is reluctant; Juliet is too young, not quite fourteen, and besides Paris had better see if she will have him. An opportunity will arise that very night, for the Capulets plan to give a ball. As the scene ends, Capulet gives a servant a list of guests to be invited.

The servant, who cannot read, asks Romeo to read the list of invitations. On it is the name of the fair Rosaline, Romeo's mistress. Benvolio dares Romeo to test his theory — that his affection for Rosaline will disappear if only Romeo will look at other girls — by crashing the Capulet party. It is a dangerous suggestion, considering the feud between the Montagues and Capulets.

A very humorous scene, between Lady Capulet, the old nurse, and Juliet, introduces Juliet to the audience. The scene now turns to a street approaching the Capulet house. Romeo, Benvolio, Mercutio, and other Maskers are on their way to the party. Romeo still glories in his melancholy, but he engages in a fierce battle of wits with Mercutio, who proves a worthy opponent. Mercutio delivers his famous Queen Mab speech.

In the Capulet house old Capulet is gleefully trying to make the party a success. As Romeo is watching the ladies, his eye falls on Juliet — Rosaline is put forever from his mind. He has been smitten with love at first sight, and so it seems has Juliet. Tybalt recognizes Romeo as a Montague and starts a quarrel. Capulet intervenes: Romeo has done nothing incorrect and, though uninvited, is a guest in the house. Romeo now approaches Juliet, who flirts with him, and their meeting ends in a bold exchange of kisses.

The second act also begins with a sonnet prologue, after which we see Benvolio and Mercutio trying to rouse Romeo, who has scaled a wall into the Capulet orchard. Romeo sees a light in Juliet's window, addresses a magnificent love poem to her, and is then astonished when she comes to the window to express, very daringly, her love for him. When the balcony scene ends the lovers are irrevocably united in love. But Juliet has not been swept away with physical desire; she returns to the balcony to tell Romeo that she desires marriage. Although Romeo had not considered this possibility, he agrees. He goes off to meet his confessor, Friar Laurence, as day breaks.

The friar is gathering herbs on the hillside. Romeo asks the friar to marry him to Juliet that day. Later, arrangements are made with Juliet's nurse, and the scene changes to the orchard where Juliet awaits word from Romeo. The nurse arrives, teases her, then announces the appointment at the friar's cell. Juliet goes there, meets Romeo, and they are married, the wedding itself not taking place on stage.

The next day the weather has turned hot — quarrelsome weather — and Benvolio and Mercutio are conversing. Tybalt enters seeking Romeo, whom he has challenged for crashing the ball. Mercutio quarrels with him. As Romeo attempts to beat down their swords, Tybalt lunges beneath Romeo's arm and slays Mercutio. Romeo then slays Tybalt.

Back in the orchard Juliet again awaits news from the nurse, who enters and leads her to believe that Romeo is dead. She then reveals that it is really Tybalt who is slain. Juliet, unreasonably upset, addresses a brilliant diatribe against her husband; however, when the nurse agrees, she reasons that Romeo must have killed in self defense. In the meantime Romeo has fled to Friar Laurence's cell. The Prince has banished him from Verona. Romeo, who cannot bear the thought of leaving Juliet, threatens suicide. The friar persuades him that life is not unbearable and arranges for him to spend the night with Juliet and consummate the marriage.

Paris now presses his suit, and Capulet agrees to marry his daughter to Paris the following Thursday. After their wedding night, Romeo and Juliet play another great love scene on the balcony, and Romeo flees to Mantua. Lady Capulet tells Juliet that she is to marry Paris; Juliet refuses. Her mother and father insist, and there is a dreadful quarrel.

Juliet goes to the friar for advice; he offers her the desperate plan to take a sleeping potion that will imitate death. Then when she is in the tomb, Romeo, he believes, can rescue her. Juliet takes the potion and her "body" is discovered by the nurse. The blow is a terrible one for the parents, who must now change the wedding into a funeral.

Balthasar, Romeo's servant, arrives in Mantua with the terrible news; the friar's letter explaining the desperate plan has gone astray. Romeo vows to lie in the tomb with Juliet, buys poison from an apothecary, and hastens to the graveyard. Paris has come there also to

16

place flowers on the grave. He accosts Romeo, whom he suspects of desecrating the tomb; they fight, and Paris is slain.

Romeo enters the tomb, drinks the poison, and dies. The friar hastens to the tomb after he learns Romeo is there and arrives just in time to see Juliet awaken. He explains what has happened and tries to take Juliet away, but she will not go. Frightened, he runs away. Juliet remains to take a last kiss from her lover's lips and plunges a dagger into her breast. Capulets, Montague, Prince and all arrive at the scene, seeking explanations for the horrible tragedy. Finally the two old men agree to end the feud and cease the awful bloodshed. They will erect golden monuments to commemorate the immortal love of Romeo and Juliet.

Sources of The Play

The first mention of the feud between the Montagues and Capulets can be found in Dante's *Divine Comedy* in the Purgatorio (vi, 106-8) where their civic disorder is mentioned as one of the reasons for Italy's social chaos. But the elements of such stories of separated lovers originated in the Greek romances and in their imitations in the Renaissance. In 1554 an Italian author, Matteo Bandello, published his novella *Romeo e Giulietta* in which the basic story is outlined. Pierre Boaistuau adapted this Italian source into French in 1559, and this French version was later translated by William Painter for his collection of stories in the second volume of *Palace of Pleasure* in 1567. However, the French version had stimulated a popular English rendition in 1562: Arthur Brooke's *The Tragical History of Romeus and Juliet*. This story of Romeo and Juliet is Shakespeare's main source. Unlike the other versions, Brooke's story was written in verse and had an immediate appeal. The basic lines of the plot are closely followed by Shakespeare, and characterizations such as the Nurse and Prince Escalus are basically similar. But there are several significant differences: (1) Mercutio in the Brooke poem is less a friend of Romeo's and more a kinsman of the Prince's; (2) Shakespeare's Tybalt is shown in earlier scenes, thus enhancing his dramatic importance in the scene in which he is killed; (3) Friar Laurence is generally viewed by Shakespeare as more sympathetic (in his preface Brooke viewed the Papist priest as the villain); (4) Romeo's melancholy in Shakespeare is more developed and motivated; (5) and finally, in Shakespeare, the intensity of the love of Romeo and Juliet and their "saintliness" is new. There are other differences important in showing Shakespeare's emphasis, but these are five clearly significant changes from the source to the tragedy itself.

The World of *Romeo and Juliet*

One of the great enchantments that a good work of literature offers is a chance to "escape." Such "escape" does not mean avoiding the realities of one's daily existence but rather deepening one's concern with those very realities. A good piece of literature presents perennial truths about human existence that have changed little in the three thousand years since Homer. The educative process of "escape" begins and ends in the little world of the particular literary work. This little world, or microcosm of the larger world, has a life all its own, and in the masterpieces, a vitality greater than any we might know in the larger world. In a very real sense, then, *Romeo and Juliet* has its own world that we must penetrate before we can understand the meaning of the tragedy. Consequently, in the beginning, the student will find it helpful to think for a moment about that world he will soon enter. Of course, such a little world will have various levels, but there are two general areas that the student can immediately recognize: (1) the physical world of time and space in which the characters move and (2) the psychological and emotional world created by the characters themselves (and, especially in *Romeo and Juliet*, revealed by the language of the characters).

The Physical World

The tragedy of Romeo and Juliet takes place in a real place in a real time. That is, Shakespeare does give the work a setting and an overwhelming sense of time. Although he was following a source, Shakespeare turns space and time into dramatic agents in the tragedy, and the student should therefore be aware of these physical elements. First, Verona is the setting. It is the Italy of the early Renaissance or possibly High Middle Ages, and the tremendous prestige of family and the highly sophisticated and formal codes of society are evident throughout the play. Verona is a city state, with a Prince. There is no King. This concept of the individual small state emphasizes the social disorder caused by the feud of the Montagues and Capulets. For the great families rule society, and, therefore, the marriage of their children in an obvious economic factor in the shaping of their society. The world is further shaped by the religion of the place, Roman Catholicism as embodied in the benign Franciscan priest, Friar Laurence.

This priest has inherited the scholastic teachings of the Schoolmen derived primarily from Thomas Aquinas. Like another medieval priest, Roger Bacon, he is scientist as well as cleric. Such a traditional combination is dramatized in the play through the use of the Catholic sacraments of confession and marriage, through the beneficent plots of the Friar, through the herbs and drug, through his ultimate spiritual aims in bringing the lovers together, and finally in his revelations at the end. In Shakespeare's own time, for example, such a stage effect as Romeo's and Juliet's confessions to a priest would have been exotic. Shakespeare therefore was fully aware of the significance of each aspect of his setting.

The sense of time is overpowering in the tragedy. Shakespeare reminds us early that it is late July in Verona: a very hot time in a hot place. Before Mercutio is killed by Tybalt, Benvolio cautions him to beware because the heat of the afternoon provokes such quarrels. The knowledge of the hot July night enhances the audience's awareness of love in the Capulet garden. But Shakespeare's use of time is more specific than a general atmosphere. It is a feeling of speed which dominates the dramatic action of the plot (and therefore the characters) from the very beginning. In order to understand this sense of time more clearly, the student should see how fast the events occur in the accompanying chart. Here he will note how the entire action of the plot covers only five days. It is a mark of the early Shakespeare's maturing powers of craftsmanship that he can compress all the dramatic action into this time and make it believable.

Time in *Romeo and Juliet*

Sunday Morning — The servants fight, and the Prince restores order.

Sunday Afternoon — Capulet and Paris talk; Romeo reads the guest list of the Capulet feast.

Sunday Night — Juliet and Romeo meet at the Capulet feast, and later in the Capulet garden (balcony scene) where they agree to marry.

Monday Dawn — Romeo and Friar Laurence plan the wedding.

Monday Afternoon — Romeo and Juliet are married; Mercutio is killed, and Romeo kills Tybalt and is banished by the Prince.

Monday Night — Capulet agrees for Juliet to marry Paris on Thursday morning; Romeo and Juliet spend their nuptial night together.

Tuesday Dawn — Juliet says farewell to Romeo and then learns that she must marry Paris on Thursday.

Tuesday Morning — Juliet hears from Friar Laurence the plan by which she can pretend death and then flee with Romeo to Mantua.

Tuesday Afternoon — Capulet is so pleased about Juliet's reversal and decision to marry Paris that he accelerates the date of the marriage to Wednesday.

Tuesday Night — Juliet takes the sleeping potion; the Capulets work through the night on the wedding preparations.

Wednesday Dawn — Paris arrives with musicians to wake Juliet; Juliet is found and thought dead.

Wednesday Morning — Juliet is taken to her tomb.

Thursday Morning (probably) — Romeo learns from Balthasar about Juliet's "death," and he buys poison for himself.

Thursday Afternoon (or early evening) — Friar Laurence learns of Friar John's mishap.

Thursday Night — Romeo enters the tomb, kills Paris and then himself; Juliet awakens, kills herself.

Friday Dawn — The families are reunited over the dead bodies of the lovers.

The World Shaped by the Characters

The world of *Romeo and Juliet* is a world shaped, simultaneously and antithetically, by love and hate. The hate is the result of the feud of the Montagues and Capulets, a hate destroying the society of Verona. It is a hate that can reach to the lowest level, as we see in the opening scene when it is the servants of both houses who start a fight. It is, further, a hate that can produce a character entirely its product, Tybalt. Tybalt's rage and search for revenge twist the plot so that finally he forces Romeo to kill him and therefore damns the lovers away from the world of Verona. On the other hand, as Friar Laurence realizes, the lovers with their frank acceptance of their feelings can redeem through love the hate destroying the social fabric of Verona. The love of Romeo and Juliet themselves is the very moral center of the play. Proof of this center can be ascertained by the lyric heights of their love scenes, from the encounter at the Capulet feast to the final scene in the Capulet vault.

It is sometimes hard for a student to accept as psychological truth the ideal love of a fourteen-year-old girl and a boy hardly older. Ideal love, as it was understood in the Renaissance, has its roots in Platonism, especially in the concept of the "ladder of love" by which the Renaissance understood that loving the single body of the beloved finally led to embracing the universal love of the One, or God. Love did not end in fulfillment, in sexual intercourse. It simply began there; there was an intensity of love for which a physical act was not sufficient. Physical love was certainly the basis for ideal love, but the idealism of love, as Shakespeare's contemporaries, Spenser and Sidney, showed, demanded a moral and spiritual element before it could truly transform. The Petrarchan lover of the sonnets that flourished in the 1590's — the time of the composition of *Romeo and Juliet* and of Shakespeare's own sonnets with their fascinating variations on the Platonic concept of love — was himself a product of this whole tradition of ideal love. Such lovers often suffered and fashionably so, as Romeo does at the beginning of the tragedy. But the intent behind the suffering, at least in the greatest Petrarchan sonnets, was a moral transformation caused by the power of ideal love, which may or may not have been fulfilled in sexual love.

The sense of moral transformation is the obvious direction of the world of *Romeo and Juliet*. The whole of the plot twists and winds to the final scene in the Capulet vault where the moral effect of the ideal love of Romeo and Juliet is to bring about a spiritual transformation in Verona itself. Such a plot of love and hate, exhibiting the power of idealism in love, teaches, more clearly than a sermon, the old moral truths. Our real world, with its loves and hates and daily need for redemptive sacrifice, is fully reflected in such dramatic action. Tragedies are never congenial but, as here, they are deeply satisfying because the moral basis of human existence, disturbed and threatened, is, nevertheless, capable of being redeemed from hate and chaos. The irony in the play is that redemption occurs not in the expected official areas of the state and church, the world of Verona, but in the ideal love of two young people for each other. As always, Shakespeare has dramatized in the imagined little world of the tragedy the deepest concerns of that larger world which we call the real world.

Atmosphere and Theme

The theme of *Romeo and Juliet* is a consuming love. It is a story of hatred overcome by that love, old hate versus young love, taking no thought for the past or the future. And this love ends in "love-devouring death".

The atmosphere is one of passion and swiftness, full-blooded passion and rash swiftness. Consuming love calls for haste — "Gallop apace, you fiery-footed steeds" — and cannot brook delay. "From nine till twelve is three long hours." The whole play is in a hurry — speed into marriage, speed into banishment, speed back to Juliet, speed in another quarter to get Juliet married to Paris, speed to kill whoever steps in the way and speed to commit suicide when life suddenly seems not worth living. Romeo's haste makes him happy in his marriage, and immediately thereafter unhappy in his banishment, for had he not so precipitately gone for Tybalt's blood he would never have been banished. *Romeo and Juliet* is a play of whirlwind and storms, full of angry feud, tremendous passion and sudden death. Like Othello, Romeo loves "not wisely, but too well".

Even when things are going well there is a sense of impending tragedy in the air, a grim foreboding that makes happy folk mistrust their happiness. The first Prologue speaks of "A pair of star-cross'd lovers" before the play proper starts. The first scene of the play shows how affairs are like powder waiting for a match, and there are those about only too glad to bring one. There is a nameless dread before Romeo has ever set eyes on Juliet.

> My mind misgives
> Some consequence yet hanging in the stars
> Shall bitterly begin this fearful date
> With this night's revels and expire the term
> Of a despised life closed in my breast
> By some vile forfeit of untimely death.

After they have met, both have a presentiment that their love shall end in disaster. Romeo comes to marry Juliet with a challenge to fate on his lips — "Then love-devouring death do what he dare". And Juliet, as she looks on Romeo (alive) for the last time, admits

> O God, I have an ill-divining soul!
> Methinks I see thee, now thou art below,
> As one dead in the bottom of a tomb.

These hints of tragedy increase the suspense (and the irony) of the play.

Yet now and again the rush and hurry, the dread and confusion stop, and there shines forth a tender beauty, appropriately enough in scenes of still moonlight — "That tips with silver all these fruit-tree tops".

It is significant that there are no fewer that eleven operas based on *Romeo and Juliet*. The reason is obvious — there are so many different emotional shades, such variety in tone colours.

Most of Shakespeare's tragedies end on a note of hope, and this, the first, strikes the pattern of the rest. The lives of these lovers are burnt up, but the final effect of the play is not wholly pessimistic. It would have been had their deaths *increased* the hatred of the Montagues and Capulets. But at the end the heads of these two houses shake hands over the "poor sacrifices of their enmity". The tragedy has left things better than they were at the start of the play.

Summaries and Commentaries
by Act and Scene
ACT I · PROLOGUE

Summary

A Chorus, probably a single figure dressed in formal robes, quiets the noisy, newly assembled audience by announcing in formal verse (an Elizabethan sonnet) the three great themes of the play: Fate, Society, and the Love of Romeo and Juliet. The setting is Verona, Italy. Two families, the Montagues and Capulets, have wrecked the social structure of their city through mutual hatred. Now their offspring, Romeo Montague and Juliet Capulet, fall in love. But this love is "star-crossed." Fate will lead "the fearful passage" of the lovers' private passion to publicly revealed death. This "passage," summarizes the Chorus, is "the two hours traffic" of the tragedy to which "patient ears" should "attend."

Commentary

The opening speech brilliantly announces the subject of the play, the "death-marked love" of Romeo and Juliet, and the three forces which will determine the direction of that love. The lovers themselves stand surrounded by the great public stage of Verona "where civil blood makes civil hands unclean." In this way, the Chorus immediately establishes the very resolution of the play. The death of Romeo and Juliet, a death in which private love triumphs over public hatred, acts as a sacrifice which atones for "their parents' rage" and unites the two families and brings civil justice to Verona. Over all, however, is the brooding force of Providence, acting through Fate to bring about these ironic but regenerating ends: social and political justice. The Chorus emphasizes the force of Fate by building suspense through the use of premonition (premonition is a device Shakespeare uses throughout this tragedy by which he forecasts the outcome of future events) and of words like "fatal," "star-crossed," "misadventured," and "death-marked." An Elizabethan audience, believing in astrology and the occult, would give its attention immediately to the Chorus. In the same manner, hearing the social theme, the audience would have turned with more belief because, as Shakespeare knew, the audience of his day would accept the tragedy of romantic love such as Romeo's and Juliet's *only* if it were established in a recognizable social context.

The tone of the Chorus' speech is august and serious, suited to the tragic occasion of all three themes. Shakespeare used the device of the single Chorus several times in his plays, but nowhere is it modeled more clearly on its stern Greek antecedents. Its dignity is enhanced here by the formal economy of an Elizabethan sonnet of fourteen lines, with its three precise quatrains and concluding couplet, in all of which not a single metaphor appears. But the austerity of this sonnet stresses another important key to the play: Shakespeare's language in which heightened rhetoric and lyrical forms express "the fearful passage of their death-marked love." The Chorus' final address to the audience is one of the few places in Shakespeare's plays where the actual playing time of a Shakespearean drama is given. The call for patience is the last attempt of the Chorus to quiet the audience and prepare them for the action. The Chorus, acting a little like Fate itself, has made clear *what* will happen; now the audience must "attend" to *how* the tragedy will happen.

ACT I · SCENE 1

Summary

Sampson and Gregory, two servants of the Capulet family, enter armed and complaining about a recent encounter with the Montague servants. Sampson declares he will not do menial work, "not carry coals," by which he means that he will not be humiliated by any Montague servant. Gregory teases the slower Sampson by retorting that if they did carry coals, they would be colliers. This word "colliers" and the tone of the banter turns to the puns "choler" and "collar" which in turn lead to Gregory's mocking of Sampson's fighting ability. Sampson catches Gregory's tone and returns the fun by announcing: "I will take the wall of any man or maid of Montague's," meaning that he would take the clean side of the street near the wall and push the other into the filth of the street. Gregory reminds him that the quarrel is only between men. But Sampson launches into a series of sexual puns which compare the act of swordsmanship and fighting to the act of physical love. Sampson will show himself a tyrant because, having fought the men, he will "cut off" the heads of maids, or their maidenheads, and Gregory, Sampson continues, can take that remark in any way he will. The maids, says Gregory, will "take it in sense that feel it." Sampson replies that these maids shall feel him while "I am able to stand" (Elizabethan slang for erection of the male phallus) and " 'tis known I am a pretty piece of flesh." Gregory responds, and the two keep up the jokes until two

23

Montague servants, Abraham and Balthasar, actually appear. Gregory, continuing the puns despite the appearance of the enemy, makes the phallic reference: "Draw thy tool," to which Sampson replies: "My naked weapon is out." But he immediately starts to flee. Soon recovering, however, he provokes the quarrel by biting his thumb at the rival Montague servants, an obscene insult. Both sides are hesitant to fight, Sampson humorously seeking a legal base before he will start. Then Gregory sees Tybalt, a nephew of Lady Capulet, approaching, and he eggs Sampson on, deliberately provoking Abraham. They fight but before Tybalt arrives, Benvolio, a nephew of Montague, enters and attempts to break up the fray. Tybalt misinterprets Benvolio's act of peace and immediately, on arriving, attacks Benvolio with: "What, drawn, and talk of peace! I hate the word/ As I hate hell, all Montagues, and thee." The street battle continues as the other followers of both Montague and Capulet enter. Then, the other citizens, weary of the bloodshed on Verona's streets, enter to beat down both sides. When Capulet, entering, hears and sees the fray, he calls for a sword, but his wife mockingly calls for his crutch. Similarly, Lady Montague restrains her husband when they enter and see the battle. At this moment appears the highest representative of political justice in Verona, Prince Escalus, with his attendants. He begins to speak to these "rebellious subjects, enemies to peace" but cannot be heard. He angrily calls both sides "beasts" and commands them, "on pain of torture," to throw their weapons on the ground. Then he turns to Montague and Capulet and reminds them that now for the third time their "civil brawls, bred of an airy word" would have disturbed "Verona's ancient citizens" and have caused the citizenry to take up swords "cankered with peace, to part your cankered hate." The Prince in his office as ruler then lays this injunction on both rival families: another disturbance and each shall die. Parting the two, he leaves with Capulet and the stage is cleared except for Benvolio, and Montague and his wife.

Benvolio then explains to old Montague how the fight began. Lady Montague wonders about her son Romeo and where he was during the fray. Benvolio answers in a rather lengthy speech, startlingly different in tone from the preceding action. Benvolio had risen before dawn that morning and, walking on the edge of the city, had seen Romeo, who, however, avoided Benvolio's company. Benvolio, using wordplay unlike any so far in the drama, decided to leave him to his "humor." Montague verifies such acts of Romeo's by stating that many mornings recently Romeo has been up before dawn, weeping, and then, after sunrise, stolen back home where he locks himself in "and makes himself an artificial night." Such action, they all know, is the sign of melancholy, and Montague makes the warning that acts as a premonition in the tragedy:

> Black and portentous must this humor prove,
> Unless good counsel may the cause remove.

Montague has, in fact, sought the source of this melancholy in order to cure his son but to no avail. Then Benvolio sees Romeo coming. He offers to try to find out the source of the melancholy if the mother and father will retire. Romeo enters and, in a few swift lines, it is immediately clear to the audience that he has "love melancholy." Romeo is the doting lover who has lost all sense of time or even place. He sees the weapons and asks if there was a struggle; then, typical of his state of melancholy, he changes and says that he has seen it all. He then elaborates on such "brawling love" and "loving hate" in a series of rhetorical passages that climax in his definition of love and its paradoxes. Benvolio asks whom he loves. Romeo's answer is not so much a refusal to name the woman as rather to lament her chastity. Benvolio wisely advises Romeo not only to forget her but deliberately to "examine other beauties." Romeo answers that seeing other beauties will merely remind him of the surpassing beauty of his beloved. They leave with Benvolio's promising to make Romeo forget.

Commentary

This crucial first scene is really divided into two parts: (1) the street battle and (2) the introduction of Romeo. The first part of the scene clearly develops that great theme of the play introduced in the Chorus' remark, "where civil blood makes civil hands unclean." Shakespeare skillfully shows how deeply the feud between the two ancient families has penetrated when he opens the scene with the servants, themselves, battling. Even the lowest level of society has been affected. It is obviously a feud that for years has rived the social structure of Verona when, finally, neutral citizens must rush in to police their brawling. The climax of the first part is the Prince's entrance. His speech underscores this state of affairs. The political order is threatened, and a sacrifice of love is needed in order to redeem it from the destructive hatred of the families of Montague and Capulet. The heads of both families, despite their immediate reaction, easily allow their wives to restrain them, and it is clear that they too would prefer peace. But, like all feuds allowed to fester, this hatred has passed beyond their control. Only an act of gratuitous love can redeem them and their society.

In this first part Shakespeare also observes the decorum that obtains in all his plays. The clowns, in this case Sampson (whose name forms a pun on the Biblical Samson) and Gregory, speak in prose and represent the lower levels of society. Their clowning is used in several ways. First, they serve as a contrast to the austere speech of the Chorus, immediately engaging the audience in their horseplay and puns. Secondly, they embody the social theme in their vivid insults and swordplay, clearly rendering in action what thematically the Chorus has established. The very fact that they (1) are armed (although with the small swords and shields typical of Shakespeare's day) and (2) possess a bravado obviously practiced over the years, carries to the audience the feeling of feud, of emergency, and of potential danger. Further, the speed with which they encounter their deadly enemies, the servants of the Montagues, portends the terrible speed by which Romeo and Juliet will fall in love and be swept to their doom. Finally, the sexual jokes and obscene gestures of these clowns begin one of the most important movements of the tragedy: the counterpoint of sexual realism, later developed by Mercutio and the Nurse, to the idealistic love of Romeo and Juliet. Their references are perhaps to a crude form of sex, but they embody one answer to the crucial question of the play, the definition of the love between Romeo and Juliet. The contrast here, in the beginning, permits the audience to see that Shakespeare is offering an ironic definition of this love from the start. Love may conquer all, Shakespeare seems to say, but there will be an ironic context around that love, even to the point of pain and death. The clowns' references to maidenheads and "tool" and "naked weapon" are a way of reminding the audience in the beginning that love necessarily has many levels, even the brutality and vigor of physical sex.

It is significant that the audience first learns of Romeo from his mother, a character of few lines, who, at the end of the play, will die from sorrow over his banishment. Shakespeare manages a very delicate transition in tone as he turns the focus to Romeo. Suddenly, from a world of brawling and hate, Benvolio and old Montague are describing scenes that are both lyric and pastoral. It is abrupt, but the drama of Romeo is quite engaging enough. At first the audience twice learns of dawns associated not with birth and light but with darkness and solitude; and the father uses a simile of the worm-bit bud that is never fulfilled. Therefore, early, Shakespeare has directed attention to fatalities latent in Romeo's career. Both Romeo's friend and his father know that he is sick with black bile, or melancholy, a disease the Elizabethans knew from their medical texts and lore. The father has a premonition of its danger; seeking "artificial night" instead of day may be fashionable, but the father knows it can lead to disaster because it can ignore the realities of the daylight world, the world of Verona. Romeo then appears like Hamlet, brooding; and as in that drama, a friend is sent to test him. Romeo clearly demonstrates all the symptoms of love melancholy. He is the doting lover of comedy, like Biron in *Love's Labour's Lost*, and meant to seem equally ridiculous. He has seemingly lost track of time and space. He has heard the brawling but could not respond. Benvolio understands this tyrannical nature of love but attempts to divert the dangerous flow of melancholy. Romeo's answers are as vague as a madman's. Shakespeare emphasizes this quality by use of sharp stichomythic dialogue (stychomythia is a form of repartee used in Elizabethan drama and derived from the classical drama, usually a line-for-line series of retorts, often in the form of antithesis) and in a speech which confuses the recent brawling with his own love, by use of a series of oxymora (182-187) (oxymoron is a figure of speech that brings two contradictory terms together, usually for emphasis). Then, in a series of paradoxes, themselves developing this deranged tone further, Romeo defines love as "a smoke raised with the fume of sighs" but "being purged, a fire sparkling in lovers' eyes." It is significant that when Benvolio asks the woman's name, Romeo is equally vague. It is his ideal love, rather than mere names, that interests him (as ironically later, the name will be all important). The woman has refused his love because she wants to be chaste. Romeo cannot even speak to her in terms of love or "bide the encounter of assailing eyes." She cannot be seduced as Danae by Jupiter, by "saint-seducing gold." She is, in short, the mistress of the Petrarch sonnets being written by the hundreds in the year this tragedy was produced. As in the first twenty of Shakespeare's own sonnet sequence, so here Romeo laments: "For beauty starved with her severity/ Cuts beauty off from all posterity." But when Benvolio asks him to forget her and to think of other women, Romeo is horrified. His ideal concept of love will allow no such betrayal. True to the Neo-Platonic heritage of such ideal love, Romeo announces that all beauty will simply remind him of the one true beauty of the world, his mistress. The very important fact, therefore, that Shakespeare clearly demonstrates for the audience in this first scene is that Romeo not only is in love but that *he is in love with the idea of love*. It is a passion that has overruled his daylight world. He has heard the brawling but even though he is the heir to the house of Montague, he has done nothing. His love melancholy has set him apart from the public world of Verona. This melancholy may be as artificial as the language describing his feelings, but the power implicit in such passion is as real as it will be at the end in the darkness of the Capulet vault. From the beginning, Shakespeare has masterfully prepared his audience for that final scene of passion, love, and death.

ACT I · SCENE 2

Summary

On a street in Verona, Capulet meets Paris, a nobleman who is a cousin of Prince Escalus. They are both returning from the judgment of the Prince on the recent feud. Both Capulet and Paris wish for an end to the ancient quarrel. Paris then inquires about his suit for Juliet's hand. Capulet refuses, as before, on the grounds that Juliet is barely fourteen years of age. She is also his only heir and child. Further, old Capulet will not agree until Juliet has shown her choice: "My will to her consent is but a part." That very night he is giving a feast. At this feast Paris can see all the beauties of the city and judge Juliet among them. Capulet hands a guest list to a servant, telling him to inform the guests of the time of the feast at his home. The servant, left alone with the list, clownishly reveals his ignorance of reading and approaches Benvolio and Romeo, who have just entered. At this moment Benvolio is giving Romeo the advice of the Elizabethan medical texts on how to eliminate dangerous melancholy: "one fire burns out another's burning." Romeo is to get some new infection of love and thereby purge the old. Romeo answers with typically vague nonsense and is lamenting his "whipped and tormented" condition when the servant comically thrusts the list at him. After some wordplay, he reads the guest list for the Capulet feast. Three significant names appear: Mercutio, Tybalt, and Rosaline. In a joking dialogue with the servant, which reveals a Romeo not so melancholy as before, the identity of the host is learned. Hearing the name of Rosaline, which he has now learned is the name of Romeo's love, Benvolio sees an opportunity to put his theory of purging melancholy into practice: "Compare her face with some that I shall show/ And I will make thee think thy swan a crow." Romeo's reaction is genuine horror. In an elaborate conceit, he compares his love with the holiness of religious faith. Benvolio reminds him that a comparison with other girls can make a difference. Romeo agrees to go to the feast just to see Rosaline.

Commentary

This scene is considerably shorter than the previous one and demonstrates Shakespeare's fondness for swift contrasts. Here the plot moves *backward* to let the audience know that Paris has sought Juliet's hand, and *forward* to announce the feast at which Romeo and Juliet will meet. Here, also, is an important revelation of the character of old Capulet. He deeply loves his only heir, his young daughter, and at this point will give her at least partial freedom to choose her mate. The episode of the clown-servant reminds the audience again of the use of comedy in the first two acts to contrast the fatal movement of the tragedy, ironically symbolized in the clown-servant himself, who performs that twist of fate which will get Romeo to the Capulet feast.

The latter part of this scene returns to the theme of Romeo's ideal of romantic love. Benvolio's method of curbing the dangerous flow of passions elicits in Romeo an outrage that finds its perfect expression in the highly artificial conceit that Romeo's false eyes would be "transparent heretics" which paradoxically often drowned, i.e., in tears, but "could never die." The rhyming couplets of both speakers add to the artificial tone, but the involved comparison of "devout religion" and Romeo's eyes when they have viewed another beauty besides Rosaline is the apex of Romeo's version of artificial courtly love where such comparisons of religion and love occur. When we meet this religious image for romantic love again, the basic passion supporting the conceit will have deepened in degree if not in kind.

But already the character of Rosaline — who never appears in the drama at all — has functioned to present a Romeo capable of the deepest passion of love. Shakespeare, as always, has not merely told his audience such a fact. He has demonstrated it in the action and dialogue, especially here in the elaborate complexities of the rhyming lines and extravagant conceits. A character capable of such an elaborate concept of ideal love is perfectly capable of falling in love at first sight. Romeo is therefore psychologically receptive to fall in love with Juliet at first sight, at the Capulet feast.

28

ACT I · SCENE 3

Summary

In a room in the house of Capulet, Lady Capulet and the Nurse summon Juliet. Lady Capulet first sends the Nurse away because her talk with her daughter is private, but remembering how intimately the Nurse is connected with Juliet, she calls her back. The Nurse confirms her intimacy by recalling in a long speech how Juliet and the Nurse's dead daughter Susan were born in the same year, and also she recalls the very day Juliet was weaned — the day of an earthquake — and her husband's sexual jest on that day when Juliet fell down and then got up, seemingly responding to the husband's joke by not crying. The Nurse is so delighted by the ribaldry of this remark that she repeats it until Lady Capulet and finally Juliet tell her to be quiet. The Nurse quiets down but only when her full affection for Juliet is revealed: "Thou wast the prettiest babe that 'er I nursed:/ An I might live to see thee married once, I have my wish." Lady Capulet retorts by saying that marriage is exactly her subject and turns to Juliet asking her what she thinks of marriage. "It is an honor that I dream not of," replies Juliet. With her practical interests, the mother replies that many women of Verona are mothers at fourteen and that she herself had Juliet at such an age. In brief, she says, Paris has asked for your hand. Juliet does not answer immediately. Instead, the Nurse and Lady Capulet remark what a good choice Paris is. Lady Capulet, in a long speech, develops this praise of Paris' good looks. This speech is quite artificial, progressing in rhyming couplets, and employing the same type of elaborate metaphysical conceits — one comparing Paris' face to a book — as did Romeo in the previous scene. The artificiality of Lady Capulet's language is contrasted by the Nurse's low sexual wordplay that Juliet will grow "bigger" by Paris. When Juliet finally answers, she is obedient but careful:

> I'll look to like, if looking liking move:
> But no more deep will I endart mine eye
> Than your consent gives strength to make it fly.

Then a servant calls them all to the feast which has already begun.

Commentary

This short scene effectively contrasts to the two previous scenes the world of the women of Verona. In Lady Capulet, however, the audience would recognize the same concern with the public scene. She knows that Juliet must make a good marriage, and her long speech praising Paris, in its euphuistic or deliberately stylized language, stresses just that code of manners which her daughter must obey. From the beginning, Lady Capulet has been rather curt and demanding. Unlike her husband, she is not interested in Juliet's own choice. As for most mothers of the time, marriage is, for Lady Capulet, a worldly transaction in which Juliet is an economical commodity: "So shall you share all that he doth possess,/ By having him, making yourself no less." She is concerned with the formal demands of Verona society, and the very artificiality of language in her long speech emphasizes those values of formal society to which Juliet must conform, as she herself did. Lady Capulet, therefore, represents one side of the world of Juliet.

The character of the Nurse, however, represents a natural, more informal aspect of Juliet's world. Both women have trained the young Juliet, but it is the Nurse who has shown the deeper affection for the Capulet heiress. The Nurse is one of the most important characters of the tragedy. It is not merely that she serves as a confidante and foil in Juliet's love for Romeo. It is, more significantly, that she forms, with Mercutio, the great realistic contrast of bawdy and physical love to the idealizing of passion to be found in the love of Romeo and Juliet. Her very first words reveal Shakespeare's use of this character: "Now by my maidenhead, at twelve years old,/ I bade her come." The audience will soon realize that only at twelve could the Nurse have been a virgin, and she clearly is laughing at herself with this remark. In a tragedy of virginal love, the Nurse then provides an irony that gives the play an air of total reality. Yet she is a character in her own right. Her long speech, in which she recounts first the birthdays of Juliet and Susan (and incidentally sets the time of the play in late July) and then the episode of Juliet's weaning, is rightly considered one of the marks of the maturation of the young Shakespeare's style. It should be contrasted with the artificiality of Lady Capulet's later speech about Paris to show the moral differences in their various influences on Juliet. Here Shakespeare has given blank verse the flexibility and rhythms of prose — the shifts in tone and breaks in phrase that clearly reveal character — without losing the formal rhythm of the iambic pentameter. The audience sees the Nurse's genuine sorrow over Susan's death and her own humility: "She was too good for me." But the character's essential bawdry — a deliberate shaping by Shakespeare — is the point where the language serves the theme. The Nurse stresses the physical nature of Juliet when she first describes the weaning of the girl (rubbing wormwood, a bitter herb, on the wet nurse's breast, was a traditional method of weaning in Elizabethan times). Having given rather specific details of the little girl's revulsion, she then relates the episode of Juliet's fall. Economy is the mark of any great dramatist, and such an episode reveals Shakespeare's early genius for construction. The joke is that Juliet's sexual nature will one day betray her, and the child, on hearing this, stops her crying as though she understood the premonition the joke involved. "Thou wilt fall backward when thou hast more wit," says the Nurse's husband, referring to sexual intercourse. The audience remembers the low sexual jokes of Sampson and Gregory, and the Nurse keeps the tone by comparing the bump on the little Juliet's head to a cockerel's testicle.

Juliet, therefore, far from being naive and childish, has had a thorough training in the realities of the social codes of Verona and the sexual nature of her existence. At fourteen, she possesses the perception of a woman. She is fully aware of the dangers and delights of love and marriage in Verona. It is natural, therefore, that she is silent when her mother first speaks of Paris, and when the two older women who have instructed her in the realities praise the young man. It is a mark of her maturity that she does not respond until her mother asks a second time. Her answer carefully shows her obedience but, simultaneously, it reveals her own mature awareness that she must observe before choosing. Thus, Shakespeare brilliantly ends the scene with a key dramatic preparation for the encounter of Juliet with Romeo. Juliet will be looking "to like, if looking liking move." She, too, is psychologically receptive, therefore, to finding her mate. She is prepared to fall in love at first sight. The two women who have trained her have commanded her to do just that, to fall in love — with Paris. Fate, however, has another destiny in store for the young Juliet.

ACT I · SCENE 4

Summary

On a street in Verona, after night has fallen, appear the young bachelors, Romeo, Mercutio, and Benvolio, with maskers, torch-bearers, and others that make the scene festive. In contrast to the world of women in the previous scene, here are lively, witty young men who are about to enter the Capulet feast. As maskers, they could visit the feast socially, but like all impromptu visits, they must make a speech of apology for their visit and then do a figure dance or "measure" while others hold torches to show off the performance. Later the uninvited maskers are expected to mingle with the invited guests. Benvolio suggests they dance and leave: "We'll measure them a measure, and be gone." But love-sick Romeo cannot endure the idea of dancing; he will merely hold a torch. Mercutio shows his genuine friendship for Romeo by trying to entice him to dance and to enter the party mood. Romeo, in an elaborate series of puns and wordplay, announces finally: "Under love's heavy burden do I sink." Mercutio answers with a sexual pun about "burden" to which Romeo answers that love "is too rough,/ Too rude, too boisterous, and it pricks like thorn." Mercutio reveals his cynical, mocking attitude toward love by retorting in sexual puns that stress the realism of physical love: "If love be rough with you, be rough with love;/ Prick love for pricking, and you beat love down." With typical nonchalance, he then turns to put on his mask. But deciding that he is ugly enough without a mask and does not need one, he turns with the others to enter. Romeo will not dance; others can "tickle the senseless rushes with their heels" (a reference to the light straw that all Elizabethan aristocrats kept on their good floors). Mercutio tries again to draw Romeo into the gay mood, suspecting the effects of such black melancholy. "Take our good meaning," says Mercutio. But Romeo has dreamed a bothersome dream. Mercutio now launches into one of the most famous speeches of the play, the Queen Mab passage. Queen Mab is the fairies' midwife, and her small size is magnificently revealed by the petite dimensions of her coachmen, horses and chariot. In this manner "she gallops night by night" through the minds of lovers, courtiers, lawyers, ladies, parsons, and soldiers. But what she brings, says Mercutio, is the deception of dream and fantasy, the very nature of Romeo's love melancholy, his romantic idealism. Romeo dismisses him, and Mercutio answers: "True, I talk of dreams,/ Which are the children of an idle brain/ Begot of nothing but vain fantasy." The obvious lesson that Mercutio intends is missed by Romeo; and when Benvolio calls for them to enter the feast, Romeo suddenly has a terrible premonition that disaster awaits him, "some consequence yet hanging in the stars." which will bring his death. His melancholy has become suddenly real. Using a traditional metaphor, he calls on Providence to watch over him: "But He that hath the steerage of my course/ Direct my sail! On, lusty gentlemen!"

Commentary

The name symbolism of Mercutio can be found at the end of *Love's Labour's Lost* (a comedy similar to the first two acts of this tragedy): "The words of Mercury are harsh." But there is also the idea of "mercurial" as we use it today: wild, fiery, impulsive. Certainly the character, with his volatile nature, serves as foil to the dreamy Romeo. His use of sexual puns underscores that function, and his generally cold, realistic outlook on love between man and woman sets up one more movement to the counterpoint of sexual realism already commented upon. But Mercutio is more than a foil. He is a genuine friend of Romeo's. Time after time he attempts to direct his bachelor companion's emotions away from the dangers of love melancholy toward the freer view of love that is his own. The climax of this friendship is the long description of Queen Mab.

One of the great passages in all of Shakespeare's plays, it recalls the world of *Midsummer Night's Dream* and, in its comprehensive view of the professions of men, Jaques' speech in *As You Like It*. The magnificence of the description is in part due to the delicate precision with which Shakespeare can paint Queen Mab's retinue. The effect is not unlike a brilliant water color, except that its basis is kinesthetic imagery, or images of motion. Quickly, Mercutio takes the audience across the various levels of mankind deceived by dreams and fantasy. Yet, whatever the beauty of the passage, its purpose is never lost. Romeo the idealist can learn a lesson framed in some of the loveliest language Shakespeare ever wrote. After this scene, the audience will delight in every appearance of Mercutio and consequently feel the full pathos of his death. But Romeo hardly hears the lesson of Queen Mab. This scene, which has given the audience one more view of Romeo's almost stubborn passion of love, ends with his premonition. The "stars" reference recalls the initial speech of the Chorus. Similarly the audience would recognize the theatrical convention of foreboding before an event as a key to the final outcome of that event. Suddenly in the premonition Romeo's rhetoric has become real as he sees the vision of his own death. A will stronger than his own has been revealed to him, and he obviously recognizes the heavy hand of Fate when he calls on Providence to guide him.

ACT I · SCENE 5

Summary

The Capulet servants are taking the remains of the dinner away, and the musicians preparing for the dance to come, when Romeo, Benvolio, and Mercutio enter as maskers. The comic antics of the servant-clowns again furnish a relief to the action on the higher level of the aristocratic characters. Also, the bustle and noise helps to add a realistic dimension to the activities. Lord Capulet welcomes all, joking that all women refusing to dance will be accused of having corns. He welcomes the maskers, as was the social custom of the day, and then bids the dance begin. Dashing about, he gives orders for more light and for quenching of the fires because the room, with all the dancers, has grown hot. (This last is an English touch since, in reality, it is July in Italy.) Turning to his cousin, he jokes about their younger days when they were maskers. In the midst of all this activity, Romeo sees Juliet and asks her name of a servant who, strangely, does not know it. He falls instantly in love. In a long speech, he rids himself of the inertia of his former state and resolves that he never learned to love until that night. But at that moment of new love, the old hatred returns. Tybalt, the proud, aggressive cousin of the Capulets recognizes Romeo and takes his appearance at the Capulet feast as an insult to family honor. When he tells old Capulet, however, he is rebuked and told to hold his place. Capulet, in fact, has heard fine things of the young Montague:

> He bears himself like a portly gentleman;
> And to say truth, Verona brags of him
> To be a virtuous and well governed youth:

Above all, the code of hospitality demands that a host never insult a guest in his home. When Tybalt refuses to be still, the audience sees old Capulet when his temper is brooked. His tirade against Tybalt is amusingly interspersed with pleasant remarks to dancers as they glide beside the two men. Tybalt rushes off, but not before he has announced that he cannot control his passion of choler if he stays. He vows revenge for this insult.

Yet, framed in this scene of hate is one of the great scenes of love in Shakespeare: the first meeting of Romeo and Juliet. Together, their first remarks of fourteen lines form an Elizabethan sonnet. From these lines, which compare their first encounter to that of pilgrim and shrine, the audience learns that Romeo's masking attire is that of a religious pilgrim. The courtly nature of the dialogue recalls the elegance of Shakespearean high comedy in which the lovers debate their love. The light, bantering Mozartian tone continues until the Nurse interrupts them, saying Lady Capulet, whose watchful eye has probably taken in everything, wants her. From the Nurse, Romeo learns that Juliet is a Capulet. Benvolio admonishes the bachelors to leave, and although Capulet invites them for a little buffet supper, they leave and he goes to bed. Juliet cautiously probes the Nurse for Romeo's name, finally sending her to find out. When she returns with his name, Juliet breaks into those paradoxes that both lovers repeat throughout the tragedy, the content of which becomes increasingly real. Her love is a monster, "prodigious birth of love it is to me,/ That I must love a loathed enemy." When the Nurse asks what she is mumbling, she lies and says that she is merely repeating what she has just learned from a dancer. The guests have all gone, and they, too, leave the stage.

Commentary

The last scene of Act I has been anticipated for three scenes, and it rightfully forms the climax of the first movement of the tragedy. At the feast, Romeo and Juliet meet and fall in love. The activity of the household adds that element of social scene in which the private love of the two young lovers will grow. In fact, they can never escape its intrusion. Their few exchanged words are surrounded by the hurly-burly of a party and by Tybalt's hatred. Shakespeare clearly intends just such an effect. The comic servants in the beginning, the effusive welcome of Capulet (contrasted to the silence of Lady Capulet), and the jokes of the two old Capulet cousins provide those elements of low comedy in which the high wit of Romeo's and Juliet's sonnet-encounter will find its right balance.

The Elizabethan audience believed in a theory of humors that was both medical and psychological. Generally, there were four humors of the body: blood, phlegm, choler (yellow bile), and melancholy (black bile). From these four physiological humors came four personality types in which each of the four humors repectively dominated. Of course, a reasonable man would have all of his four humors functioning in the right proportions. But excesses in each humor produced a special psychological type. Excess of blood, for example, meant that a character was extraordinarily sanguine and bold. Too much phlegm meant that he was listless, or in our contemporary word, phlegmatic. As we have already seen, the Romeo of the first four scenes is a man burdened with too much melancholy. He, therefore, shows all the personality traits of the excess of black bile. Finally, too much yellow bile, or choler, resulted in a personality perpetually angry and aggressive. Such a character is Tybalt.

It is impossible for the audience to form a rounded view of Tybalt's choleric character because, like the wise and moderate Benvolio, only one aspect of him is revealed. As old Montague and Romeo's friends know, remaining in one's excessive humor was extremely dangerous. It is logical, therefore, that Tybalt, as a revenge character, should precipitate the crisis which will lead finally to the death of both Romeo and Juliet. One cannot simply explain him psychologically by pointing to his sense of family honor. As Capulet, in his praise of Romeo, shows, the feud is no longer so important to either side. Both sides seek peace. Tybalt is, in fact, a tiresome bore to Capulet, a "goodman boy." But, like Romeo, he is marked by an uncontrollable passion, as Tybalt himself reveals. When he is leaving old Capulet, he is angry and petulant because he has not been able to kill Romeo at the Capulet feast. Because the humors were believed to be somehow related to the movements of the stars, they figured in the astrology of the day. Like Romeo and Juliet therefore, Tybalt is "star-crossed" and Fate will use his death by Romeo to urge its own designs. His humor of choler will destroy him and the lovers, but ultimately Providence will turn this hate to redemptive love.

It is ironic that Romeo's first words at the sight of Juliet — words so monosyllabic and alliterative that the speaker is literally open-mouthed with wonder — reflect that same light-darkness imagery the audience had associated with his love for Rosaline, and in the same rhyming couplets. But, in fact, it is the same passion that now grips Romeo. He may say: "Did my heart love till now? Forswear it, sight!/ For I ne'er saw true beauty till this night." But he is using the very same exaggerated language in swearing his new love. In fact, the hyberboles that dominate the first four lines are of the same kind as those used in describing Rosaline. Another irony is the fact that here Romeo is doing just what Benvolio wanted him to do: purging love melancholy through falling in love with another. Shakespeare underscores this irony when Romeo in lines 50-1 describes Juliet in the very simile that Benvolio has used to describe the effect of his method of purging (Scene 2, lines 90-1). The repetition is deliberate and cutting. Where then is the difference between the expressions of the old and new loves? It lies in degree, not in kind. Romeo is still in love with love, but the intensity of the new love can be measured by those hyperbolic images of light and darkness in the first three lines, an intensity that may begin in artificiality but moves quickly into a realm of belief.

> O, she doth teach the torches to burn bright!
> It seems she hangs upon the cheek of night
> Like a rich jewel in an Ethiope's ear;

A further irony that unites the old and new loves of Romeo is the fact that the imagistic pattern of the sonnet which the newly met lovers recite to each other is none other than Romeo's when he vowed to Benvolio that his eyes would be "transparent heretics" if they even looked at another. It is the comparison of romantic love and religious devotion that John Donne was later to use with such powerful effect in poems like "The Canonization." It was a comparison that formed an integral part of the medieval and Renaissance tradition of courtly love poetry, especially as found in the Petrarchan sonnet. The religious

35

imagery, springing naturally from Romeo's costume, serves two main purposes: (1) it serves to make the ideal love of the two young people sacred and pure by association (even though their secular use of such terms as "pilgrims," "shrine," "devotion," "palmer," and "saint" allows the tension of wit to emerge between the two poles of the different religious and secular meanings) and (2) it serves to isolate the lovers even more in the midst of the bustle and activity of the Capulet feast. The idealism of religion, even though brought in by wit and parody, reinforces the idealism of the newly found love. The audience would immediately understand both the wit and the idealism as Romeo gently touches Juliet's hand and begins to woo her in true Renaissance style, indirectly and through metaphor, i.e., through the wit of high comedy. It becomes, of course, a kind of duel of wordplay in which sharp intelligences and puns serve for swords.

Romeo attacks with the bold metaphor: "my lips, two blushing pilgrims." Juliet modestly retorts by referring back to his hand, reminding the strange young man that "palm to palm is palmer's kiss." When Romeo asks if saints do not also have lips, Juliet replies that they are for prayer. With logical thrust, Romeo demands that lips have the same privilege as hands or "faith turn to despair." Juliet does not agree but simply answers: "saints do not move, though grant for prayers' sake." Romeo catches the cue immediately and kisses her. When Juliet then says her lips have sinned, Romeo, without asking, kisses her again and says: "Give me my sin again." At this point the encounter is in the genre of high comedy; there are no passionate outbursts. There is simply the lightness of kissing, as Juliet says mockingly, "by the book" or rules of such courtship. The very formality of the Elizabethan sonnet itself accents the control of their feelings and their complete and rational awareness of what has happened. Romeo may have been converted into action, and the very action of that conversion measures the seriousness of this new love, but thus far it is the love of comedy and not of tragedy. Romeo has become a burlesque of the old doting Romeo the lover. As a consequence, the audience admires Juliet all the more when it sees her ascendance over Rosaline. But the grace of their sonnet-dialogue might have occured in any Shakespearean comedy where, after witty debate over love, a happy marriage blesses the lovers. Suddenly here, however, with all the terrible swiftness that characterizes this play, Romeo learns the fatal truth from the crude Nurse, who even tries to bargain Juliet the heiress off on the strange young man: "I tell you, he that can lay hold of her/ Shall have the chinks." For the rest of the scene, the lovers speak in paradoxes, and this figure of speech seems to express the turmoil and bizarre nature of their passion. "My life is my foe's debt," says Romeo, the old artificiality of the first four scenes purged from the paradox by the sheer terror of the fact. But already before Juliet learns Romeo's name, she has foreshadowed her own death: "If he be married,/ My grave is like to be my wedding bed." This foreshadowing, like the premonitions, is a clear example of dramatic irony (that is, where action in the play is supposed to turn out one way but turns out another). The audience knows something the character speaking cannot know — her death — and sees the irony of it. When Juliet learns Romeo's identity, she screams out the paradoxes that must now rule her life like a dreadful monster or new-born prodigy:

> My only love sprung from my only hate!
> Too early seen unknown, and known too late!
> Prodigious birth of love it is to me,
> That I must love a loathed enemy.

Romeo had come to the Capulet feast hoping to glimpse his love, Rosaline, and to feed his love melancholy with greater beauty. Juliet, commanded by her family, had come to the feast to look at her intended, Paris, and hopefully to find love. What each found was more terrible and more wonderful than either could have dreamed: the love of each for the other, making a sum greater than their two parts.

ACT II · PROLOGUE

Summary

The figure of the Chorus steps before the audience once more and, like a Greek chorus, both recapitulates the action and at the same time comments on its future possibilities. He speaks again in a formal Elizabethan sonnet, but now the language is more figurative and echoes the Petrarchan love sonnets. Rosaline, he says, has been replaced when she is "with tender Juliet matched." Romeo is still "bewitched by the charm of looks," but it is Juliet he loves. He longs to tell her so, a fact that the audience might surmise from the ending of the last scene, but which is told here in preparation for the scene in Capulet's garden. There is the almost unsurmountable problem of the families, how to "steal love's sweet bait from fearful hooks." But where there is such passion, a way will be found: "passion lends them power, time means." For such an extreme and abnormal situation, certainly revolutionary in the society of Verona, an extreme solution will be found so that the lovers will meet. Thus, the extremity of their passion and the dangers it entails will be mollified by an equally dangerous but sweet answer: Romeo will steal into Juliet's very garden and expose his life. Those moments in the garden of intense joy will temper all dangers "with extreme sweet."

Commentary

Most critics agree that this speech is hardly necessary. It merely repeats what has occurred and implies the next bits of action. Its language is more the language of the euphuistic rhetorical lover (note the rather hackneyed metaphor of the first two lines; the use of chiasmus — a figure of speech in which a criss-cross effect of antithetical terms is used — in the last line; and the prevailing antithesis of structure with alliteration and assonance). But without question the Chorus still retains its old dignity. It still functions as a reminder of the forces of Fate, of powers outside the action that are perfectly capable of controlling the action without ever appearing. It serves to set the first steps of the lovers in the broad perspective outlined in the first speech of the Chorus: Fate and Society. Without this perspective, the great love duet soon to appear would lose its reality for the audience. Romeo and Juliet, as we shall see, are never completely isolated, although their love finds most beautiful expression in a poetry born of their seeming isolation.

ACT II · SCENE 1

Summary

Romeo has run ahead of his bachelor friends because he needs to recover himself from the swift, momentous events of the last few minutes. But he cannot go forward; he must see Juliet again. Using the medieval theory of the elements as a base for his wit, Romeo sees that his "dull earth," his body, must seek its natural elements, its "center," Juliet. It must sink to that element and, hearing Benvolio calling, Romeo leaps over the wall into Juliet's garden. Mercutio thinks Romeo has left them merely to get to sleep. But Benvolio has seen him jump the wall (not knowing it is into the Capulet garden). Mercutio calls and, in a lively bachelor mood, conjures Romeo as though a magician. The words of conjuration all recall the Romeo before the Capulet feast. They all refer to his love melancholy: not only "humors," "madman," "passion," "sigh," but also the techniques of the Petrarchan poet, "ay me" and the rhymes "love" and "dove." Romeo should speak to "my gossip" Venus, or give a nick-name to Cupid, who shoots so well that he shot King Cophetua, the hero of an old ballad who was destroyed by love. When he gets no answer, Mercutio says that "the ape" or the fool is "dead" and he'll have to conjure him back to life. For that, Mercutio will need the greatest words of magic. Therefore, he describes Rosaline's eyes, high forehead, lip, foot, leg, "quivering thigh" and finally all the regions "that there adjacent lie." Benvolio, knowing Romeo's idealistic passion, warns Mercutio to be careful lest he anger Romeo. But Mercutio will not be stopped. In some of the bawdiest of all passages in Shakespeare, Mercutio continues in the liveliest of spirits with his puns, wordplay, and *double-entendres*. This will not anger him, announces Mercutio but if I raised a spirit in "his mistress' circle/ Of some strange nature," and I let it stand there until "she had laid it and conjured it down," then Romeo would be angry. My invocation, says Mercutio, is honest; I only want to raise Romeo up. The entire speech, needless to say, with all the Elizabethan puns with which Shakespeare's audience would be quite familiar, is not about conjuring so much as about the sexual act. Benvolio hardly listens but instead respects Romeo's desire to be alone, as he thinks. His love is blind, says Benvolio and he seeks the dark for consolation. Mercutio picks up the cue of "blind" and away he goes, transforming Romeo's ideal love into the crudest of sexual references. If his love is blind, it will not "hit the mark" or be shot in the right direction. Further he imagines that Romeo will "sit under the medlar tree" and "wish his mistress" were fruit from that tree, as young girls, laughing alone, understand that fruit to mean female genitals. Reaching a zenith in this ribaldry, Mercutio makes a pun on the sound of "O" which he equates with "an open *et cetera*" or, again, the female genitals. Romeo was, of course, to be the "poperin pear," an Elizabethan expression for the male phallus. Then, just as abruptly, Mercutio bids the listening Romeo farewell, preferring his small but realistic truckle-bed to the vast field (i.e., Romeo's idealism) to sleep in. (Mercutio is probably referring here to a proverb of the day.) Benvolio agrees it is hopeless to seek their bachelor friend when he does not want to be found.

Commentary

Without a clear understanding of what he is doing here, the audience might see the scene as merely an excuse for Mercutio's antics and think Shakespeare is simply being vulgar. The meaning of this scene depends heavily on the love duet in the next. Mercutio is focal. His wit and jokes all revolve around the realism of physical love. It is impossible for him to comprehend more than the physical dimension of human love, and it is natural, therefore, that he be cynical and even cold toward romantic sentiment of any kind. Or so it seems. Again, one must remember that Mercutio is truly the friend of Romeo. He wants to help him out of the dangers of his "humor" of melancholy which, as Mercutio and the Elizabethan audience know well, can lead only to a passion which must result in death. How else to "teach" his friend except by frank jokes about what Romeo idealizes? Certainly the exquisite love duet, the most celebrated scene of idealistic love in Renaissance literature, demands the irony that the bawdry sets up if the duet is to be humanly recognizable. Shakespeare was a master of construction in his early years; and he recognized fully that a few strokes in another direction would only strengthen the running current of the love duet. For that reason the Chorus has reminded the audience of the powers of Fate and Society, which surround the young lovers. Now Mercutio adds another countering element, the jokes about physical sex, which with their mocking tone, contrast to the sincerity in the lovers' expression of devotion. Ironically, Mercutio cannot know how deeply Romeo is in love. When he sees Romeo again, however, he will see that something has transformed him. But now, Romeo, hearing all the taunts, realizes that he has already entered a sphere of reality that the Mercutio of the jokes can never enter. "He jests at scars that never felt a wound," says Romeo and turns to seek Juliet. He is still not in control of his passion, and he is still in love with love. But all his extravagance of expression and emotion will find its natural "center," as Romeo says at the beginning of this scene, in Juliet. It is she who will provide his love with reality, who will offer him a communion of love more frightening, more swift, and more transporting than any dream of love melancholy.

ACT II · SCENE 2

Summary

On the other side of the wall, Romeo listens to Mercutio and Benvolio leaving. Then looking up into the moonlight night, he sees Juliet appear at one of the windows. Knowing that Juliet cannot hear him, he praises her. This soliloquy, or speech to himself, shows the audience the depth of Romeo's feeling for his new-found love, but it also demonstrates that he is still the same lover, in love with love. The conventional subjects of the idealist Petrarchan lover appear in the usual exaggerations and hyperboles. (A hyperbole is a figure of speech that employs exaggeration for the purposes of emphasis.) Juliet is more radiant than the moon; her eyes are stars that outshine any in the heavens. It is natural, that Romeo think of these aspects of the night: he is looking up at a Juliet framed by clouds passing across a bright moon in a sky studded with stars. Again, he is looking up, and Shakespeare makes the posture a part of the whole scene. Romeo sees each action of Juliet's. She leans her cheek upon her hand. Like all true lovers, he longs to be there secretly, as her glove, just to touch her. Juliet's first words reflect the love she feels, and the words "Ay me" are melancholy. (Ironically, they would remind the audience of Mercutio's use of the same phrase when he tried to conjure up Romeo.) She does not know that Romeo is below. Her speech, therefore, is completely natural and without the guile of most young girls, as she herself recognizes a little further on. At the sound of her voice, Romeo's love rises above the conventional images of his first soliloquy; or rather the new images of this speech are lifted to a great plateau of emotion and intensity of experience. The image in this speech is again one of the light Juliet brings into the dark night; it is again conventional of the Petrarchan sonneteers (Juliet as an angel); and "the white-upturned wondering eyes" looking at the angel in the images are merely his, looking up at Juliet. The religious motif that first introduced the lovers is used again. Here it emphasizes the purity and isolation of the lovers as they speak. They are saints of love, cloistered in their own experience. Juliet speaks again, still unaware of Romeo. She recalls Romeo's name with sorrow: "O Romeo, Romeo! Wherefore art thou Romeo?" It is the names, their social identity, that isolate the lovers and prevent them from fulfilling their love. If Romeo will not "deny" his father, then she'll "no longer be a Capulet." Hearing this complete statement of her love for him, Romeo can hardly keep hidden. Juliet continues with that hard and rather logical method by which she pursues, as we shall see, any subject: a Montague is not a part of a man's body "nor any other part/ Belonging to a man." It is not the reality of experience such as theirs. "What's in a name?" she asks. "That which we call a rose/ By any other name would smell as sweet." "Romeo," she calls out as though her beloved were there, "doff thy name" and "take all myself." At this moment of surrender, Romeo steps forward. He, too, will surrender his name and, "new baptized," take the name of "love." He, too, will accept the social isolation of their love. Juliet, naturally, is frightened. But after Romeo once again denies his name to his "dear saint," Juliet recognizes him even though she has not heard "a hundred words/ Of that tongue's utterance." True to her realistic nature, Juliet checks out the literal situation: how did you get in this dangerous place? Romeo, true to his idealistic nature, answers "with love's lightwings." Juliet, as throughout the tragedy, sees immediately the inherent violence in the situation: "If they do see thee, they will murder thee." Romeo dismisses all the talk of danger. More peril lies, he says, in your eyes than in "twenty of their swords." With her sweet look, he is proof against her family. Further, he had rather die by their hate than have the extended death of lacking her love. Literal again, Juliet wants to know how Romeo found the garden. "By love," who, though blind, let him counsel and he in turn gave Cupid eyes. Extravagantly, Romeo declares that he would pursue her to "that vast shore washed with the farthest sea." But Juliet is more concerned with the essentials of their relationship, and, in her next speech, she comes to the point. Realizing that he has overheard her declaration of love, Juliet says that if Romeo could see her clearly — and it is significant that the lovers pouring forth their love never see each other very well in the night light — he would find a blush. I would like to dwell on form and compliment in our relationship, she says, but I cannot. At their first meeting, surrounded by the bustling formalities of Verona, they had spoken in compliment and wit, indirect forms of love. But now, with a speed that characterizes their actions from this time forward in the tragedy, Juliet gets to the point. She knows he can lie to her: "Jove laughs" at lovers' lies. But she hopes he will "pronounce it faithfully." Perhaps Romeo thinks her too easily won. She could enter into all the formal coquetry that a young girl of her class would be well trained in. But her passion has denied that social code; and she will, Juliet declares, be more faithful than the other kind of girl. "Therefore pardon me," she says; her haste was not "light love/ Which the dark night hath so discovered." Looking beyond her, Romeo begins to answer Juliet, to swear by the moon, the traditional image of the Petrarchan lover. Juliet objects; the moon is too inconstant. In fact, he should not swear at all, or, if he must, by himself "which is the god of my idolatry,/ and I'll believe thee." When Romeo starts again with an exaggerated phrase, practical Juliet stops him. She has a moment of premonition, of fear:

> I have no joy of this contract tonight:
> It is too rash, too unadvised, too sudden;
> Too like the lightening, which doth cease to be
> Ere one can say 'It lightens.'

The speed with which their passion has engulfed them is too

frightening for her literal nature. She starts to bid him farewell, using a rather involved metaphor as she leaves, the most extravagant of any figure of speech she has uttered so far. "This bud of love" in the ripe July heat, may blossom into "a beauteous flower when next we meet." Romeo cries out in anguish: "O, wilt thou leave me so unsatisfied?" Juliet replies, with a kind of teasing wit, what kind of physical satisfaction can he expect tonight? After all, she is up on the balcony. Romeo, as idealistic as ever, seeks merely the exchange of love's vows. As sharp in this witty repartee as any heroine of Shakespearean comedy, she answers: "I gave thee mine before thou didst request it." But she would like to have her vow back now. Why, says Romeo, do you withdraw it? To give it back again, she answers, continuing in a speech that shows, in its simplicity, her depth of passion for Romeo:

> My bounty is as boundless as the sea,
> My love as deep; the more I give to thee,
> The more I have, for both are infinite.

At this climactic moment, the Nurse calls from inside. She answers, but as she goes in, she tells Romeo to wait a moment. Alone, Romeo cannot believe his happiness:

> O blessed, blessed night! I am afeard
> Being in night, all this is but a dream,
> Too flattering-sweet to be substantial.

Juliet immediately returns, and her request is substantial enough. If his love is honorable, he is to send her word tomorrow by her messenger "where and what time thou wilt perform the rite" of marriage. With terrible haste, she will surrender all to him "and follow thee my lord throughout the world." Romeo has no time to answer. The Nurse calls again, Juliet, talking to both, says that perhaps Romeo means not well. He merely answers (in usual fashion): "So thrive my soul." She whispers good night and leaves. Romeo is still reluctant to leave. He has hardly gone a few steps before Juliet comes out again. She says she would love to hold Romeo as a falconer holds his falcon; or, if she were not in the "bondage" of her family, she would scream his name: "else would I tear the cave where Echo lies." The violent images, which recur in her speeches throughout the scene, and the precision and speed with which she acts, are a measure of the intensity of Juliet's passion. Romeo's answer is typically Petrarchan and gentle: lovers' tongues at night sound like music, "silver-sweet." Juliet, has a question about the time of the meeting tomorrow but, as she admits, she really has nothing to say. She merely wants his presence. He also wants to stay there in the garden. True lovers cannot part. But Juliet sees the impossibility of his lingering; it is near dawn. She would like to keep Romeo as a child does a pet bird, letting it hop about but always pulling it back by a string. "I would I were thy bird," says Romeo. "Yet I should kill thee without much cherishing," says Juliet. She leaves abruptly, as though a violent departure were the only way:

> Good night, good night! Parting is such sweet sorrow,
> That I shall say good night till it be morrow.

Romeo lingers after her departure, calling to her:

> Sleep dwell upon thine eyes, peace in thy breast!
> Would I were sleep and peace, so sweet to rest!

He finally leaves, however, going immediately, by the dawn's light, to Friar Laurence's cell at the local Franciscan monastery.

Commentary

This famous scene, most often called the balcony scene (although it is not absolutely clear how it was originally staged), is not only a high point in the poetry of the tragedy, but also in the dramatic action. Shakespeare has prepared early for the first free exchange of feelings. Delineating the love-sick Romeo and then the young Juliet amid the Capulet's social pressures, he then draws the lovers together briefly at the Capulet feast. But the formality of their language stresses their necessarily impersonal contact. An audience would need more proof of their love before it could believe in such a passion. Carefully preparing for the lyric heights through the realism developed in the two preceding scenes, Shakespeare now goes the full limit. The result is that audiences for almost four hundred years have fully believed in the romantic passion as revealed in the love duet of Romeo and Juliet. Oxford students who had read this scene so many times that the Bodleian First Folio was worn to tatters by 1664, were the prototypes for audiences and readers the world over.

Shakespeare achieves the effect of unparalleled lyricism by doing several things all at once. First, he gives to the night itself a reality of nature that his earlier plays had often lacked. In doing so, the magnificence of the Italian night is turned into a means of defining Romeo's love for Juliet. The confusion of the moon-lit heavens and Juliet begins immediately. She is a dawning, the sun itself. With her supreme light she can overshadow the moon or Diana (goddess of the moon, the hunt, and chastity) to whose retinue she belongs because of her chastity. But "the envious moon," with its dress of virgins ("vestal livery"), has the green color of unloved girls. Juliet is more: she is loved. Again, in the same speech, Romeo looks up at the figure just above him. Using an hyperbole typical of the Petrarchan tradition, he says that Juliet's eyes, at the stars' request, are twinkling in the sphere. And from his physical vantage point, they might appear as such; indeed, in the very next line, he admits he is confused about which is which. Carried away by the ecstacy of this correspondence, Romeo then takes his hyperbole to its conclusion by announcing that even her cheek would shame those stars "as daylight doth a lamp." Her eyes as stars would cause the birds to think it day because of their brilliance. But the greatest effect of the Italian night's serving as a means for defining Romeo's love comes after

Romeo has heard Juliet's voice for the first time. Juliet, framed by the Italian night, becomes at that moment a creature of those heavens that he sees moving behind her. She becomes at once Mercury, the messenger of the pagan gods, and a Christian angel such as one might see in Italian Renaissance paintings of the Annunciation, a Botticelli or Fra Angelico.

> O, speak again, bright angel! for thou art
> As glorious to this night, being o'er my head,
> As is a winged messenger of heaven
> Unto the white-upturned wondering eyes
> Of mortals that fall back to gaze on him
> When he bestrides the lazy-pacing clouds
> And sails upon the bosom of the air.

The magnificence of this passage lies not only in its linguistic achievement and the imcomparable success of the hyperbole, but in the dramatic aptness of the image. It is his sense of love that Romeo is describing, something the audience has seen developing since he first wandered on the families' fray in Scene 1. His concept of his passion is angelic, idealistic, but raised to a point of intensity at which these terms do not exist. Of course, the lesson of Mercutio still lurks in the background; such passion is loaded with dangers, even with death. But, for the moment, Romeo has found the fullest expression of his passion of love. The religious motif in the passage, echoing the first meeting of the two lovers, strikes the right note for Romeo's concept of his passion: divine and holy.

If the night serves to reveal Romeo's love, it also serves to isolate the lovers. The privacy of their love can release itself in the quiet night-world of the Capulet garden as it never can in the daylight world of Verona. In fact, this great theme of love is seen precisely in its isolation from the forces of Society and Fate, forces that will finally destroy the love as, in return, both will be redeemed or fulfilled by the passion of love. As critics have pointed out, one of the devices by which Shakespeare dramatizes this isolation is the imagery of light and darkness. Throughout the play, Juliet appears to Romeo as light amid darkness. In his first words about Juliet, she is brighter than the torches at the Capulet feast. The scene is completely built around the idea of light and darkness, a concept that a lover so totally committed as Romeo would naturally embrace. Nothing counts but his love; she is the only true light in the darkness of the world. It is her uniqueness that makes her sacred and worthy of complete surrender. Juliet, far more practical, nevertheless feels the same way. They are isolated. Her way of approach to this transforming but dangerous state is by practicalities: Romeo's name; the danger of his present position; the "lightning" violence inherent in all their acts (violence to the whole body politic of Verona); his attitude toward her frank proposals, the practical details of their wedding the next day. She seems in this pragmatic concern hardly a woman swept by passion, yet in her speech about her boundless love, she tells the audience that she is. In her similes about birds, and in her delays, she decidedly shows the audience her passion. It is precisely because she feels an isolation from society that her perceptions are full of violence. Her images, too, in this scene and later, will dwell on the same paradox: in the day-world of Verona, the lovers find darkness; in the Italian night, the lovers with consummate lyric expression find angelic light in each other and in their love. Their love, as Juliet unknowingly foresees, is like the swift flash of lightning in the night. They are light to each other in a world of darkness.

ACT II · SCENE 3

Summary

Friar Laurence, Romeo's confessor, is gathering herbs in the same dawn hours that Romeo is leaving Juliet. He peacefully and lovingly describes (and by this means, Shakespeare takes the audience down slowly from the lyric heights of the last scene) the dawning of the day. He is out to fill his basket or "osier cage" with special herbs and flowers while the dew is still upon them. Friar Laurence is the learned man of the monastery who functions as both spiritual guide and scientist (or alchemist), a traditional combination at the time of the play. Both as philosopher and scientist, he remarks on the paradoxical power of the earth to be both tomb and womb to life. There are "virtues excellent" to be found in the herbs and flowers that he is gathering. Nothing is so vile on earth that it does not have a special grace that it returns to the earth. But, equally, nothing is so good on earth that "strained from that fair use/ Revolts from true birth, stumbling on abuse;/ Virtue itself turns to vice, being misapplied." He then lifts a flower and announces that in it is both poison and medicine. From there, priest that he is, he draws a homily or short sermon about the nature of man:

> Two such opposed kings encamp them still
> In man as well as herbs, grace and rude will;
> And there the worser is predominant,
> Full soon the canker death eats up that plant.

When Romeo greets the Friar, the older man is amazed that so young a man is up so early. He soon guesses that Romeo has not been to bed all night. Yes, says Romeo: "the sweeter rest was mine." Thinking that Romeo has slept with Rosaline, the Friar cries out: "God pardon sin!" Romeo announces that he has forgotten the name of Rosaline. He jests about the mutual wound he and his enemy have given each other and that the only help is the Friar's "holy physic." The Friar is confused and reminds him that such a rambling confession will bring no absolution. Then Romeo tells to the amazed Friar the story of how he met Juliet last evening, visited her in the garden, and desires to marry her this day. With holy exclamations, the Friar remarks on Romeo's fickle nature. He even pretends to see on Romeo's cheek a stain of a tear once shed for Rosaline. It is true then, says the Friar, "women may fall, when there's no strength in men." Romeo reminds his confessor that the older man often chided him for loving Rosaline, and the wise Friar adds significantly: "For doting, not for loving, pupil mine." Romeo was not to "bury" one love and take out another. Romeo counters his spiritual father by saying that Juliet loves him as much as he does her, and Rosaline never did. The Friar answers that Rosaline knew well that Romeo was play-acting, loving by "rote" but could not "spell" true love. Yet the Friar has obviously seen in Romeo's face his new state and, more important, he sees a means to unite the deadly enemies of Verona in a wedding, therefore saving them from their mutual destruction. Romeo is now all haste. But the Friar's final admonition prophesies the future danger of their swift passion: "Wisely and slow; they stumble that run fast."

Commentary

The last of the important characters to appear is Friar Laurence. His role is roughly equivalent to Prince Escalus in that he, too, is outside of the family dispute and represents the spiritual nature of the community in which the Prince represents the dispenser of justice. The wise Friar (greatly altered from the original figure in the source) is also the instrument of Fate itself. An Elizabethan audience would immediately associate him with the old alchemists, and the herbs we see in the beginning are a clear portent of the medical power he will later use to save Juliet. His first speech is like a little sermon, and, in it, the audience would hear discussed, although in an indirect manner, one of the underlying themes of the tragedy: the danger of too much will or passion in which virtue can turn to vice. Man has free will, but it is self-destructive unless freely chosen reason controls passion. The priest never stops reiterating this theme throughout the drama. Like Mercutio, he reminds Romeo of the dangers of his passion. Romeo is up too early; this is not natural. Further, when he learns of Romeo's desertion of Rosaline, he laughingly calls on "holy Saint Francis" to witness such folly, and he proceeds to joke with Romeo about his "tears" and the fickleness of love. Finally, it is Romeo's "doting" (a word that to the Elizabethan implied a kind of madness) about which he worries. Even though he finally agrees to marry the two young lovers, he reminds Romeo and the audience of the dangers involved in such speed. Friar Laurence is the vital link from their isolation to the outside society of Verona. His blessing of their marriage may be the first step toward linking them to the rest of the world, but as an instrument of Providence, he knows the terrible powers of Fate to bring about the ends of Providence. He therefore warns the young Romeo.

ACT II · SCENE 4

Summary

Later the same morning, Benvolio and Mercutio are looking for

Romeo on the streets of Verona. Benvolio reports that Romeo did not come home. Mercutio remarks what his actions have already proven; he fears Romeo will go mad with love. Then Benvolio announces that Tybalt has sent a challenge to the house of Montague. When Benvolio says that Romeo will answer it, Mercutio laments the fact. Romeo cannot fight. He is already dead with love: "stabbed with a white wench's black eye; shot through the ear with a love-song; the very pin of his heart cleft with the blind bow-boy's butt'shaft." Tybalt is no mean adversary, he continues. He is "more than the prince of cats," referring to the Beast Epic of *Reynard the Fox* in which the cat's name was Tybert or Tybalt. Mercutio, ever the realist, mocks Tybalt's precise manner of dueling (popular among Englishmen of the day) imported from Italy and France, the various terms denoting an ideal fight rather than a real one. He denounces the new breed, mocking their nice tones ("A very good whore!") and the "new form" which he puns with the English term for school-bench. He also puns the French "bon" with the English "bones," to emphasize his mockery of affected manners.

At this point, Romeo arrives on the scene. Mercutio, at his height of mockery, merely turns to Romeo, supposing that he is as afflicted with love melancholy as before. Romeo is a dried fish without his Rosaline, lacking his "roe," the first syllable of her name. "Now is he for the numbers that Petrarch flowed," says Mercutio, recalling the fashion of the extreme Petrarchan love sonnets. Mercutio catalogues all the women of history famed for love, cheapening each as he thinks Romeo might. Then he applies his same satiric thrusts about the Italian and French forms to Romeo, finally asking about his night out. Romeo pretends nonchalance, but it is clear from the witty retorts he gives Mercutio (both sides of this quick repartee having sexual overtones) that he is a new man. Romeo can exaggerate language at any time, and his special thrust to Mercutio — "O single-soled jest, solely singular for the singleness" — delights Mercutio into pretending to faint. Calling their verbal duet "the wild-goose chase," the merry bachelors continue until Mercutio, viewing a transformed Romeo, cries out: "Why is not this better now than groaning for love? Now thou art sociable, now art thou Romeo." The old Romeo, "this drivelling love," was like an idiot, "a great natural," that wanted to hide his bauble in a hole. The sexual puns ("bauble" was another word for the male phallus) disturb Benvolio. But Mercutio, as always, cannot be stopped in his high spirits. His "tale" cannot be stopped "against the hair," he announces, continuing the puns. Benvolio says that Mercutio would have added too many suggestions to his story, would "have made thy tale large." No, answers Mercutio, "I would have made it short." He has "come to the whole depth of my tale; and meant, indeed, to occupy the argument no longer." Then in walks the Nurse, followed by the Capulet servant, Peter, who is carrying her fan. She is indeed "goodly gear," as Romeo describes her. Mercutio senses a new target: "A sail, a sail!" The Nurse reveals her desire to affect manners by commanding Peter to give her the fan which a lady of modesty always wore before her face when approaching strangers. Mercutio greets her by wishing her good evening, although it is still noon. To the Nurse's surprise that it is already so late, Mercutio answers with his usual sexual puns: "'Tis no less, I tell you, for the bawdy hand of the dial is now upon the prick of noon." The Nurse pretends amazement at his frankness (but not his joke) as Romeo mollifies her. She in turn asks for young Romeo; and when, after witty wordplay, Romeo reveals himself, she asks to speak privately with him. Benvolio and Mercutio find the invitation excruciatingly funny. Mercutio calls her "a bawd," or procuress. When Romeo wants to know what he has found so funny, Mercutio says "No hare, sir," unless it is a rabbit in a lenten pie, that is, a rabbit without meat. Having punned again, ("hare" was pronounced like "whore" in Elizabethan times) off Mercutio goes, singing a song about a hoary old hare, the meaning of which would be obvious to an Elizabethan audience. He and Benvolio leave, with Mercutio ironically applying to the Nurse the "lady" refrain of a popular Elizabethan ballad about a virtuous woman. The Nurse pretends anger at such flippance with her. Mercutio is, says Romeo, "a gentleman, Nurse, that loves to hear himself talk." The Nurse drops all her affectation and swings into the vernacular. She'll "take him down." She is "none of his flirt-gills" or "skains-mates," terms that referred to loose women and seamstresses whose reputation for virtue was low. Then she turns angrily on Peter, who says in his defense that he has seen "no man use you at his pleasure." If he had, his "weapon should quickly have been out." He is the same coward as Sampson of the first scene. The Nurse turns to Romeo and tells him to respect Juliet and not "lead her into a fool's paradise." After some banter in which it is clear to Romeo that he cannot talk clearly to her, Romeo makes the plans to be married that afternoon at Friar Laurence's cell. After giving the Nurse some money, which she pretends not to want but does accept, Romeo also tells her that his man will send a ladder of rope so that he can sleep with Juliet that night and consummate the marriage. The Nurse chatters on about her mistress and about Paris "that would fain lay knife aboard" or, in more decent terms, would marry her. She says she teases Juliet about Paris' being better than Romeo. Then, with an odd premonition, she tells how Juliet associates rosemary, the flower of remembrance used at weddings but also at funerals, with Romeo. Romeo cannot stand her chatter and he leaves, politely asking to be remembered to Juliet. The Nurse leaves in grand style with Peter and the fan going before her.

Commentary

In all tragic romances, especially with "star-crossed" lovers, certain facts have to be carried back and forth in order to get on with the plot. But the high atmosphere of tragedy and the sublime language of such action do not always allow for such scenes to be believable. Shakespeare succeeds because he causes the two great comic centers of his drama to collide. Mercutio dominates the first half of the scene; the Nurse, the last half. In both halves the audience learns vital facts: Tybalt has sent a challenge, and Romeo and the Nurse arrange the wedding and the nuptial night. Mercutio's natural antagonism toward Tybalt will be ironically climaxed shortly, but here Mercutio is at the height of his humor. He is sincerely happy over Romeo's new-found optimism, and the joke of the affected old Nurse increases his good mood. The sexual jokes that he and the Nurse constantly refer to are again a part of the counter-movement in the tragedy that helps to contrast and define the intense passion of Romeo and Juliet. The scene, incidentally, as Shakespeare's decorum of language would demand, is all in prose except for the blank verse of Romeo's description of the rope-ladder and his hopes for the nuptial night.

ACT II · SCENE 5

Summary

Juliet, walking in the Capulet garden, has waited "three long hours" for the Nurse to return. It is noon, and the Nurse had left at nine with a promise to return in half an hour. Juliet is filled with anxiety. The staccato rhythm and shifts in speech pattern at the beginning of the scene stress her emotional state. Her feeling finds expression in the conceit that "Love's heralds should be thoughts,/ Which ten times faster glide than the sun's beams." For the swiftness demanded by true lovers, "nimble-pinioned doves draw Love,/ And therefore hath the wind-swift Cupid wings." But the Nurse is old; she cannot be "swift in motion as a ball." With an unconscious dramatic irony, Juliet says that old people feign "as they were dead" and are "heavy and pale as lead." The Nurse finally arrives, but her face is sad. Her body aches and she will not immediately give her message. Juliet is furious with her complaints and asks for a direct answer. The Nurse teases her by both praising and mocking Romeo. Juliet is not interested in the old woman's assessment of her lover. Again, the Nurse starts to complain, and Juliet tries a new tactic. She sympathizes, but finally must demand: "Sweet, sweet, sweet nurse, tell me, what says my love?" The Nurse still delays, even asking for Lady Capulet. Juliet blows up: "Here's such a coil!" or I'm ready for a fuss now. At this the Nurse relents and tells Juliet that she must go to Friar Laurence's this afternoon. Juliet blushes, and the Nurse, in sexual frankness, announces that she will "fetch a ladder, by the which your love/ Must climb a bird's nest soon when it is dark." The Nurse complains about her job as a go-between, but adds that tonight, at the consummation, Juliet "shall bear the burden."

Commentary

The purpose of the scene between the Nurse and Juliet is to demonstrate that Juliet is equally resolved to pursue her love to its end as is

Romeo. Shakespeare dramatizes this resolve in a scene that is a hodge-podge of exquisite poetry (the Venus and Cupid images) and prose, romance and earthy realism, pathos and farce. He does this in two ways: by giving Juliet a soliloquy in which she can reveal her feelings, and by using the Nurse's trick of delaying to render Juliet's true emotions under such a test. Juliet's final blush is proof of her genuine love if these earlier methods of characterizing her passion were not enough. The Nurse functions like a character out of an old Roman comedy, carrying her messages back and forth. The delaying trick is one of the oldest gags in comedy. She also acts, as Juliet clearly states, as part of the antithesis of old age to the youth of the lovers, an important counterpoint in the tragedy. Lascivious old woman that she is, the Nurse delights in forecasting the sexual pleasures of the bridal night. It is interesting to note that all the participants accept the wedding in the afternoon and the consummation at night as one.

ACT II · SCENE 6

Summary

Friar Laurence and Romeo await Juliet in the priest's cell. Friar Laurence, with evident anxiety, prays that Providence will bless the marriage and not give them later cause for sorrow. Romeo answers a hasty "amen, amen" and then announces that no sorrow can destroy "the exchange of joy/ That one short minute gives me in her sight." He defies the forces of death; after marriage it will be enough if he can "call her mine." The priest is horrified at such a declaration of absolute love. To defy the forces of mutability and change is not to understand the very conditions of life. To reprove Romeo, Friar Laurence gives him a little homily or sermon, which serves as one of the important guideposts to the meaning of the tragedy.

> These violent delights have violent ends
> And in their triumph die, like fire and powder,
> Which as they kiss consume: the sweetest honey
> Is loathsome in his own deliciousness
> And in the taste confounds the appetite;
> Therefore love moderately; long love doth so;
> Too swift arrives as tardy as too slow.

Before he can point his lesson home, Juliet enters and, as Friar Laurence notes, she walks so lightly (as a result of her desire) that she could tread on gossamer and not fall. Romeo's first greeting to her is so rhetorical and so emotional (as usual, he must define his feelings as soon as he has them) that Juliet chides him indirectly. Imagination, she says, must have substance, not words or "ornament." Only a beggar can count his worth. Her "true love" is so tremendous that she cannot use words to describe even half of it. The Friar comically ends the scene by declaring he must marry them before he will allow them to stay together alone.

Commentary

It hardly seems possible that, only a few scenes before, Romeo and Juliet met each other at the Capulet feast and then proclaimed their love in the garden. Now they are wedded, and if the play were a comedy — which the first two acts could very easily have been — it would end here, as in all Shakespearean comedies, with a wedding. But the very element of speed that has marked the courtship portends another fate for the lovers. On Sunday morning the play had opened; on Sunday night Romeo and Juliet saw each other for the first time, and, later that night until dawn Monday, they spoke their vows of love in the Capulet garden. Now, on Monday afternoon, they are married. This speed itself seems part of the atmosphere of premonition that pervades the play. It is precisely the sense of the joy to be found only in the swift movement — a pagan, Epicurean concept — that horrifies Friar Laurence, who represents, in the tragedy, the stoic-Christian principle of moderation, of reason over passion. In the surrender to the moment, Friar Laurence sees the same abandonment of reason that Mercutio saw in Romeo's melancholy. Romeo is a young man who has not learned the lesson of mutability, the law of all existence. Death is still rhetoric for him: "Then love-devouring death do what he dare." All Romeo can consider is the immediate satisfaction; he abandons himself to the moment. The Friar's little sermon strikes at the crucial problem of the play and, like the Chorus and Prince Escalus himself, gives a definitive answer, "Violent delights" will end in triumph but in triumphs short-lived. The image Friar Laurence uses is one that recurs throughout the play: the image of explosion — another variation of the prevailing pattern of light and darkness imagery — "like fire and powder, Which as they kiss consume." The explosion image, like the lightning image that is also repeated throughout the tragedy, expresses well the speed and violence that surround and finally define the love of Romeo and Juliet. But life is mutability, says the Friar. "The sweetest honey" is finally loathsome. The only way in which passion survives is under the rule of reason. The kind of love which these two have chosen, is to taunt death and tempt the power of Fate. The normal cycle of love and marriage in which children are the offspring of passion, leading to middle age and old age, cannot sustain such intensity. They must be moderate, "long love doth so;/ Too swift arrives as tardy as too slow." Like Mercutio and the Nurse, like the social forces of Verona itself, Friar Laurence reminds the young lovers of their potentially "sinful" action in viewing nothing but the idealism of their passion. Such isolation is of the purest intensity, but dangerous. His sermon at the wedding, therefore, is a clear foreshadowing of their tragic end and provides one more example of Shakespeare's intensive use of dramatic irony in the tragedy.

Play takes place in Verona

ACT III · SCENE 1 *Italy*

Summary

It is later in the same afternoon of the wedding, and as Benvolio and Mercutio walk along the public square of Verona, Benvolio remarks on the heat. It is late July in Italy, and the heat affects everyone, especially Mercutio. Benvilio warns him about the combination of the heat and the Capulets who are stirring about, all of which sets "the mad blood stirring." Mercutio, in this weather, is petulant and ready to pick a fight. He pretends, however, that not he but Benvolio is ready to fight: "Come, come, thou art as hot a Jack in thy mood as any in Italy, and as soon moved to be moody, and as soon moody to be moved." Mercutio then lists all the superficial occasions that he pretends would provoke Benvolio: a "quarrel with a man for cracking nuts"; "with a man for coughing in the street"; "with a tailor for wearing his new doublet before Easter"; "with another for tying his shoes with old riband." To this Benvolio simply replies that it is Mercutio who is describing himself and if he were like Mercutio, he would not live an hour and a quarter for any man could "buy the fee-simple" of his life or have the absolute ownership. At this point Tybalt enters. He is angry and ready to fight. When he asks for "a word with one of you," Mercutio asks him to couple it with a blow. Tybalt merely lacks an occasion, but when he tells Mercutio that he "consorts" with Romeo, Mercutio takes offense easily at the derogatory meaning of consort — a term relating to musicians — and draws his "fiddlestick," or sword. Benvolio tries to draw Mercutio away, but before he can, Romeo enters. Tybalt announces: "Here comes my man." Mercutio, punning as ever, defies Tybalt by telling him that Romeo is no servant of his. But Tybalt is already provoking Romeo: "Romeo, the hate I bear thee can afford/ No better term than this — thou art a villain." Romeo has just returned from his wedding — a fact that only the audience and Romeo know — and he tells his new cousin, Tybalt, that he has reason to love him, that he is no villain, and that he bids him farewell. Insultingly, Tybalt calls him what old Capulet had insultingly called Tybalt himself: "boy." Once more, Romeo turns away, protesting that he never injured Tybalt but loves him better than he can know. Mercutio is horrified at Romeo's seeming cowardice: "O calm, dishonorable, vile submission!" He draws his sword. He will fight the "king of cats" and take one of his nine lives. Romeo tries to prevent their fighting, and he steps between them. At this point, Tybalt thrusts his sword under Romeo's arm into Mercutio and then flees. Mercutio is mortally wounded, and his first comment is to curse both houses, the social feud that has destroyed the peace of Verona and now even the Prince's cousin, Mercutio himself. He declares that he has "a scratch" (of the cat-king who has "gone, hath nothing"). To Romeo's inane call for courage because "the hurt cannot be much," Mercutio answers in sarcasm that his wound is "not so deep as a well, nor so wide as a church door" but that "'twill serve." Tomorrow he will be a "grave" man, remarks Mercutio in his last pun. Then he turns his invective first against the houses that held the feud; then against Tybalt, "a cat to scratch a man to death!" and "a villain, that fights by the book of arithmetic!" (or by the formal rules of dueling) but who, like a coward, killed him under Romeo's arm, hardly an honorable way to fight; and finally against Romeo himself: "Why the devil you came between us?" Romeo's childish lack of realism reveals itself. "I thought all for the best," says Romeo. Romeo's idealistic appraisal of a situation has now led to disaster, as Mercutio predicted. Mercutio ignores him, and in an obvious rebuff to their friendship, he asks Benvolio and not Romeo to help him into some house. Mercutio's last remark is to curse both houses and the feud that has finally taken his life as it has threatened to destroy Verona. Romeo, left alone, sees the disgrace of his situation; the love that he had so idealized has left him "effeminate." Benvolio immediately returns to tell Romeo that Mercutio is dead: "That gallant spirit hath aspired the clouds,/ Which too untimely here did scorn the earth." Romeo's answer is a clear premonition of tragedy: "This day's black fate on more days doth depend;/ This but begins the woe others must end." Tybalt returns, and seeing him, Romeo vows revenge for "fire-eyed fury be my conduct now!" Deliberately, Tybalt taunts Romeo calling him "wretched boy" who "didst consort" with Mercutio. In the swordplay that follows, Tybalt is killed. Benvolio cries out that "the citizens are up" and that the Prince will condemn Romeo to death if he does not flee. Romeo's reply is the full recognition of the power of fate: "O, I am fortune's fool!" He flees, and the Prince soon enters. Benvolio explains the bloodshed. Lady Capulet laments the death of her beloved nephew and calls on the Prince to kill a Montague in return. Benvolio unravels the situation for the Prince, exaggerating, perhaps, Romeo's humility (and possibly with sarcasm at his seeming cowardice). Lady Capulet believes that Benvolio lies because he is a friend of Romeo. She demands the life of Romeo. The Prince reminds her that Tybalt slew his cousin, Mercutio. The punishment for Romeo, announces the Prince in rhyming couplets, is exile. Both houses will be heavily fined, and the Prince sees that in previous times he should have been harsher: "Mercy but murders, pardoning those that kill."

Commentary

This scene is the turning point of the play. All the action up to this point could possibly have been in the realm of comedy, especially the high comedy of euphuistic romances. But Mercutio's death allows for nothing but tragedy, as Romeo says in one of those speeches that Shakespeare uses throughout for dramatic irony: "This day's black fate on more days doth depend." Fate, through the force of accident, has timed the wedding day of Romeo — the moment of the consummation of love — with the murder of Mercutio. No recourse but revenge and, after that, exile, can follow. The moderation that the Friar had taught and which Mercutio himself had indicated through his emphasis on realism (a lesson Mercutio himself forgets in this scene when he follows honor and not reason) is lost in the quick movement of Fate. Tybalt's hatred, the result of his "humor," must touch the love of Romeo and Juliet. They cannot be isolated. Mercutio's dislike of Tybalt has been well planted by Shakespeare in earlier scenes, yet it is Romeo who sparks the fight that brings Mercutio's death — or rather it is his ideal and truly innocent belief that his love can bind the wounds of the feud. But the feud is not merely the result of the hot July days; it has been allowed to fester too long. The body politic is itself threatened. One important aspect of this "hate" scene is its speed. Like the love of the lovers, hate spreads swiftly in the action, and in a few moments, two men are killed and another banished for life. This speed gradually becomes, at least in the psychological impact of the tragedy, but one more aspect of Fate itself. These are the "violent ends" that the Friar had warned Romeo about, and although Romeo in action is noble and completely honorable, he recognizes the trap in which he is now caught. He is truly "fortune's fool." In killing Tybalt, he has done the wrong thing for the right reason; honor of friendship demanded such an act, but moderation demanded less "fire-eyed fury," less passion. Once more, Romeo suffers because of his own choice. But Shakespeare is very clear that, like all human actions, those of Romeo are ambiguous. He is both right and wrong, and for that ambiguity he will suffer tragically. As the audience alone knows — such a confidence in the audience is a marvelous trick of any dramatist — Romeo is caught in the terrible irony of being between love and hate, and powerless to do anything but act in the demands of both. It is true that it all might have been avoided (there are so many seeming accidents), but it is precisely the unnecessary nature of the hate, and even love, that represents the power of Fate. Lady Capulet climaxes the sense of the family feud when, true to her fierce nature, she calls for blood for her blood. The Prince's final rhyming couplets act, as do such couplets throughout the play, to bring a generalized impersonal mood to the action. After such violence, their soothing effect is like the calm after a storm.

ACT III · SCENE 2

Summary

In the Capulet garden, Juliet, not knowing the terrible events of the last scene, awaits Romeo and her marriage night. In one of the loveliest speeches of the play, she calls on the horses of the sun to return to their lodging and bring in night and the hour of consummation for their love. She then invokes night, with its "close curtain, love-performing night" in which Romeo can leap into her arms. Juliet, as the audience saw from her first scene, is direct and frank and especially here in her description of the delights of her bridal night. "Lovers can see to do their amorous rites/ By their own beauties" and since Cupid is blind, night is the best season. She then invokes night as a sober matron, "all in black," who will teach her how "to lose a winning match,/ Played for a pair of stainless maidenhoods," hers and Romeo's. Night, she continues in an involved conceit built on the Elizabethan sport of falconry, should "hood" the "unmanned blood" showing in her cheeks with its black cover. Or, night as a trainer should cover the untrained blood fluttering in her cheeks. (The falcon's eyes were covered as it sat on the trainer's fist so that he could check its fluttering or bating, a sign that the falcon — like Juliet here — is ready for the kill.) In this way her reserve will finally think the natural act of love as "simple modesty." She repeats once more her invocation to night but quickly turns to Romeo, echoing, throughout, the word "come" which suits the invocation but also indicated to Shakespeare's audience the sexual experience of orgasm. She continues this frank and rather violent evocation by suggesting Romeo's sexual posture in the night (using here another image of light in darkness and recalling the very same one which Benvolio and later Romeo had used):

> For thou wilt lie upon the wings of night
> Whiter than new snow on a raven's back.

Violently, she calls on night once more to "give me Romeo." in an elaborate conceit — whose elaborateness keeps the tone of violence — she relates Romeo to the star imagery that dominates the play from the Chorus' first speech.

> and, when he shall die,
> Take him and cut him out in little stars,
> And he will make the face of heaven so fine
> That all the world will be in love with night
> And pay no worship to the garish sun.

Again, Romeo is light to her; "cut" into little stars — a variation on the ancient idea of apotheosis or the idea that a famous hero became a star — Romeo will make darkness itself preferable to day, as can their love, Juliet seems to imply. But behind the conceit is the sexual pun "die," which, in Elizabethan times, meant not only physical expiration but also experience of sexual orgasm. The pun reinforces the ironical idea that their love, although in dark isolation from the world, is in reality brighter than the day. That is, Romeo, exhausted from the act of love, or "dead," will in his apotheosis in the heavens prove a brighter and truer light than the sun. Finally, in complete sexual frustration, Juliet cries out with all her frankness and violence:

> O, I have bought the mansion of a love,
> But not possessed it, and, though I am sold,
> Not yet enjoyed; so tedious is this day
> As is the night before some festival
> To an impatient child that hath new robes
> And may not wear them.

The Nurse enters at this moment, holding the ladder. Juliet sees her wring her hands and when the Nurse simply wails "He's dead" time after time, she assumes the Nurse means Romeo and asks: "Can heaven be so envious?" The Nurse misunderstands, and the effect here, though in blank verse, is comic. Juliet answers in a speech that puns on the words "aye" or yes and "I" after cursing the old Nurse for her "torture" in not being clear. If the Nurse says that Romeo is dead, the vowel "I" or aye or yes will give more poison than the fabled monster, the cockatrice. The Nurse, obviously stunned by the event of Tybalt's death and too stupid and insensitive to notice Juliet's face, describes in detail the gory wounds on Tybalt's body. The violent contrast between the presumed fact of Romeo's bloody death and the sexual expectation of her opening speech is too much for Juliet, and she is slowly collapsing with a "broken heart," hoping — in another dramatic foreshadowing — that she "and Romeo press one heavy bier." Then she hears the Nurse speak Tybalt's name. Juliet assumes, with almost farcical misunderstanding, that now both her husband and her favorite cousin are killed and if so, then it is time for doomsday, the Last Judgment. Then she hears the terrible truth that Romeo has "shed Tybalt's blood," her own, the blood of the Capulets. For a moment, she is overcome with horror. Her family honor has been besmirched and, like Romeo, when he avenges his family name and Mercutio in killing Tybalt, Juliet feels her family name disgraced. But the emotion is false and temporary; and Shakespeare brilliantly underlines the falsity of these emotions by using a series of oxymora in which she denounces Romeo through a series of verbal paradoxes, using finally the image of the book which her mother had used first for Paris: "Was ever book containing such vile matter/ So fairly bound?" The Nurse tells Peter to bring brandy for herself and calls for shame to come to Romeo. Suddenly Juliet reverses herself. "He was not born to shame," says Juliet. Rather, Romeo's brow is "a throne where honor may be crowned/ Sole monarch of the universal earth." The old Nurse rebukes her: "Will you speak well of him that killed your cousin?" Juliet, setting the order of her obligations straight, retorts: "Shall I speak ill of him that is my husband?" She rebukes herself for villifying Romeo and is grateful that he is alive. Tybalt, her beloved cousin, might have killed her husband; and Romeo is greater than her family. But suddenly Juliet recalls the Nurse's words about banishment and the exile of Romeo. Tybalt's death "was woe enough" but to the sound of "banished" Juliet can find "no end, no limit, measure, bound,/ In that word's death." When the Nurse asks if she will go to Tybalt's corpse to weep, Juliet replies that her tears will be for Romeo's exile. She shall "die, maiden-widowed" and, in another foreshadowing of Romeo's speech at her tomb, Juliet replies that Death, not Romeo, will "take my maidenhead." But the Nurse will bring Romeo to her bedchamber to comfort her beloved Juliet; she knows where he is. Juliet, in sudden ecstasy, gives her a ring to take to Romeo and bid him come to her for a last farewell.

Commentary

The opening speech of this scene is an *epithalamium*, one of the several verse forms that can be found in this extremely lyric drama. It can also be called a *serena*, or evening song, which a woman often sang in anticipation of her lover. But the *epithalamium*, or wedding song, more accurately describes the emotional and psychological content of the soliloquy. The first lines, violent in their call to the horses of the sun-god, Phoebus Apollo, set the tone of urgency that marks Juliet's character here as elsewhere. Spenser's great poem, "Epithalamium," has lines almost identical as the young husband longs for the delights of the marriage bed. Here the roles are reversed, and, in her most frank speech, Juliet longs for the physical joys of the sexual consummation. Shakespeare clearly dramatizes Juliet's maturity in her bold response to her own physical needs, but there is nothing vulgar or crude in her response as rendered in the speech. Above the sexual wordplay lies a genuine and ideal love for Romeo. For Juliet, as for Romeo, the sexual is but another means of expressing the intensity of it. Such speed of passion could only long for immediate fulfillment of the heavy hand of Fate. This sense of Fate returns in Juliet's intricate and violent reference to the stars; the audience would always catch the dramatic irony when both lovers compare each other to the stars. As usual, Shakespeare has made the imagery — here the light-darkness pattern — serve the purposes of characterization and theme as well as express heights of lyric poetry. But all of Juliet's rhetorical exaggeration in her repeated invocations to Night and in her involved conceit with falconry are belied by and contrasted to her final simile, comparing herself to "an impatient child that hath new robes/ And may not wear them." She is still a child of fourteen, and her deepest experiences are still those of her childhood. Only by comparing her present emotions to them can she understand these new desires. But Juliet hardly has a moment to analyze her emotions. For, with the appearance of the Nurse, she drops immediately through fear and terror to despair only to be raised slightly when she learns Romeo is alive. The comic misunderstanding merely sharpens the poignancy of Juliet's turbulent emotions. Her use of oxymora to express her feelings is both artificial and right in its violence. The final despairing surrender of her "maidenhead" to death and not Romeo is ironically foreshadowing the Gothic theme of death and the maiden that marks the final scene.

ACT III · SCENE 3

Summary

Friar Laurence enters his cell and tells the hidden Romeo to come out: "Affliction is enamoured of thy parts,/ And thou art wedded to calamity." But the Friar thinks he has good news. Romeo is not to be killed, but the Prince's "doom" or judgment is that he should be exiled. Romeo's reaction is the very same as Juliet's in the previous scene. Death is preferable to banishment. Romeo bursts into a rhetorical outpouring that carries the ring of reality to it. For once the dramatic situation is equal to his wordplay. "There is no world without Verona walls," he cries out, "But purgatory, torture, hell itself." Banishment is "death mistermed." The Friar rebukes him, as he shall throughout this scene, for his emotional outburst. He is ungrateful; he could have been condemned to death. No, says Romeo, exile is "torture, and not mercy; heaven is here,/ Where Juliet lives; and every cat and dog/ And little mouse" can look on her. But he cannot. Even "carrion-flies" may touch "the white wonder of dear Juliet's hand" or touch her innocent lips, but he must "fly" all this "heaven" where Juliet lives. He immediately seeks "poison-mixed" or a "sharp-ground knife" — a foreshadowing of the instruments by which both lovers shall die — rather than suffer banishment. He calls on the Friar, "a divine, a ghostly confessor/ A sin-absolver, and my friend professed" not to "mangle" him with the word "banished." The Friar calls Romeo a foolish man and says he will give him "Adversity's sweet milk, philosophy" for comfort. In fury, Romeo answers "Hang up philosophy!" To the Friar's remark that "madmen have no ears," Romeo retorts: "How should they, when that wise men have no eyes?" In fact, says Romeo when Friar Laurence wants to "dispute" with him about his condition, you do not know anything about the intensity of our love. Only if you were as young as I, just married, having just murdered a man, "doting like me and like me banished," could you have the right to speak and tear your hair and even fall on the ground. With that, Romeo thrusts himself to the floor, "taking the measure of an unmade grave." At this moment there is a knock on the door. The Friar thinks it is the authorities of the city who have come to arrest Romeo. While he answers and stalls the knocker, he chides Romeo for not rising from the floor. When he finally opens the door, it is the Nurse looking for Romeo. In disgust the Friar points to the floor: "There on the ground, with his own tears made drunk." Just as Juliet, says the Nurse, and then exhorts Romeo to stand up if "he be a man," for Juliet's sake. At the name of Juliet, Romeo suddenly notices the Nurse and even rises, asking what Juliet, "my concealed lady," thinks of him. The Nurse says she weeps and falls on the bed, repeating his name and Tybalt's. His name, says Romeo, like a gun, did murder her. Where he asks the Friar desperately, "in what vile part of this anatomy/ Doth my name lodge?" Then Romeo draws his sword and tries to kill himself. This is the climax of his melancholy over his exile, and the priest not only restrains him but, as though a real father, rebukes the young man. Romeo's danger, as the audience recognized from the first scene of the tragedy, is his inclination to put passion over the necessity of reason and moderation. It is precisely this surrender to passion that Friar Laurence rebukes: "thy wild acts denote/ The unreasonable fury of a beast." Friar Laurence is amazed. Romeo has learned nothing of his teaching: "by my holy order,/ I thought thy disposition better tempered." In trying to kill himself, Romeo has forgotten the logical result of such suicide, this "damned hate upon thyself": he will kill Juliet as he killed Tybalt in his fury. He is a creature of free will, with the intellect to choose his action, or at least to confront valiantly the powers of the world with the use of reason. He has a moment of choice greater than the three forces that formed him.

> Why rail'st thou on thy birth, the heaven, and earth?
> Since birth, and heaven, and earth, all three do meet
> In thee at once; which thou at once wouldst lose.

Like a catechism, the Friar instructs Romeo in what three aspects of his nature he is destroying by such acts: his "shape," his "love," and "his wit." Like a usurer, he abounds in all of them but does not make true rational use of any of them. In shape, he is like wax because he has digressed from "the valor of a man." His love is "hollow perjury" because he is killing that love he "vowed to cherish" in his marriage vows. His "wit" or intelligence, "that ornament to shape and love" is "misshapen in the conduct of them both." Using the recurring image of explosion, the Friar says such misuse is like the "skilless" soldier who keeps his gunpowder in his flask and by his "own ignorance" sets it afire and dismembers himself with his "own defense." The Friar tries further to rouse Romeo by telling him all the reasons he has for optimism. Juliet is alive; he has killed an enemy in Tybalt; he has exile as a judgment, not death; in fact, "a pack of blessings lights upon thy back." But Romeo is pouting as a child about his "fortune" and love. The Friar sounds a warning if such passion continues: "Take heed, take heed, for such die miserable." Romeo, however, seems only to listen to the last part of the Friar's long speech: Romeo is to go to Juliet's chamber that night and then flee to Mantua where he can stay until the marriage has been revealed and Romeo forgiven. Then he can return to Verona "with twenty hundred thousand times more joy." The power of Friar Laurence as a character — and Shakespeare's use of him to counterbalance the love of Romeo and Juliet — is dramatized in the Nurse's admiration: "O Lord, I could have stayed here all the night/ To hear good counsel: O what learning is!" Romeo agrees to the proposal and is revived when he sees Juliet's token of the ring. The Nurse departs, and the Friar agrees to send him messages from time to time by his servant Balthasar. Romeo ends the scene by telling the Friar how much the comfort of the older man has meant:

> But that a joy past joy calls out on me,
> It were a grief, so brief to part with thee.

Commentary

This scene complicates the plot by divulging the next stage of the action: that is, the Friar's strategem of eventually revealing the marriage and bringing Romeo back; and by using the Nurse as a go-between to bring the news of Juliet's reaction to Romeo. Such mechanical complications are necessary to the progress of the action, especially where the two central characters are separated from each other. But Shakespeare's power of construction will not accept mere mechanics as the purpose of a scene. The result is that here the audience is invited to focus on the deeper meaning of the tragedy, especially as that meaning focused in the character of Romeo. The problem that is dealt with here is Romeo's problem throughout: his passion or refusal to moderate his feelings with reason. As in other scenes, the familiar structure of antithesis appears to guide the action. Here it is not the pattern of love and hate, but age and youth. Friar Laurence is clearly held by Romeo to be his true father. It is with him, therefore, that he will reveal his deepest urges. Consequently, when Romeo throws himself to the floor and twice threatens suicide, Romeo is not play-acting but revealing a quite genuine desire. It should be said first that Friar Laurence's statements are to be taken as truth; if there is irony in their general context, it seems rather clear that Shakespeare did not mean this irony. The Friar is the voice of religion, and religion in the Elizabethan age was the authority of God speaking directly to the age. This is not to say that the Friar understands Romeo completely. To the character of the Friar (*not* to his teaching) there is, perhaps, the edge of absurdity. A man who advises philosophy to such an emotional young man is obviously a little like Polonius in his blindness to human passion. Also, the impulse to turn to dispute rather than to psychological counsel implies the overlogical framework of some of the Friar's philosophical concepts. But the truth of the Friar's remarks would have been accepted immediately by Shakespeare's audience as they saw Romeo throw himself in a childish fit to the floor and remain there even though the enemy might be at the door. So saturated is Romeo with his melancholy that he does not even notice the Nurse even though she has been standing beside him for thirteen lines of the play. Also, the audience would have noticed that before Romeo can hear all of Juliet's reaction from the Nurse, he starts to kill himself. The Friar's long speech therefore would not only be accepted but expected by Shakespeare's audience. Such a display of passion needed the philosophical rebuke that the Friar gives. Romeo is a creature of free will but he has submitted, in his freedom, that will to the forces of passion, in this case his melancholy over his exile. Without use of reason, as the explosion image tells the audience, Romeo is destined for disaster. The lesson of the Friar, therefore, is the lesson of the Prince to the families: moderation. But as Romeo himself knew — and as lovers of these lovers through the ages have known — the intensity of his love for Juliet, and hers for him, cannot be measured philosophically. It may invite dangers, but love has a joy that the lovers feel worth any sacrifice and which only the lyric heights of the poetry seem to express.

ACT III · SCENE 4

Summary

In a room in his house, old Capulet and his wife are entertaining

Juliet's suitor, Paris. Old Capulet has not had time to talk to his daughter again about Paris' proposal because of Tybalt's death (which he regrets, although he comforts himself with "Well, we were born to die"). Juliet will not see him, nor in fact, would the Capulets be up on this Monday night if it were not for his visit. Paris takes his leave but as he does, Capulet changes his mind and says that he is sure Juliet will take his hand because her father demands it. At first, Capulet sets Wednesday as the date; then he changes it to Thursday because of the proximity to Tybalt's murder. "Will you be ready?" he says to Paris. "Do you like this haste?" It will be a small wedding because of the recent events. They say good-night, and going to bed, old Capulet remarks that "it is so very very late,/ That we may call it early by and by."

Commentary

As Romeo had predicted at the death of Mercutio, events beyond his control are now set into motion. Thus, as a result of Tybalt's death, old Capulet, needing the prestige of a relative of the Prince's as his son-in-law, agrees to force Juliet to marry Paris. The accidental and coincidental forces add to the dramatic irony that Juliet is already legally married and is, in fact, at that moment of Monday night celebrating the consummation of her marriage. The force of this extra event would heighten the tragic mood that the audience has felt impending from the Chorus' first speech. The fact that Capulet chose to make the wedding date Thursday, only three days ahead, reinforces the sense of speed in the tragedy, which finally becomes identified in the audience's mind with Fate itself.

ACT III · SCENE 5

Summary

It is the dawn of Tuesday morning in the Capulet garden. Juliet and Romeo are waking in her bedroom. The nuptial night is over, and he must flee to Mantua. A bird has sounded, and as in Shakespeare's high comedies, the lovers lightly debate its identity. Juliet will not believe it is so near the light of day. (Even her father in the previous scene had not decided whether it was very very late or early.) The bird was the night-bird, the nightingale. It sings each night on the pomegranate-tree of the Capulet garden. Romeo says the bird is the lark, "the herald of the morn." In fact, he says, it is dawn and he points out to Juliet the first streaks of daylight.

> look, love, what envious streaks
> Do lace the severing clouds in yonder east:
> Night's candles are burnt out, and jocund day
> Stands tiptoe on misty mountain tops.

Juliet still refuses to accept what she now sees. This light is merely "some meteor that the sun exhales" to act as a torchbearer for Romeo on his way to Mantua. Romeo, who has for once acted practically, now

61

reverts and says: "Let me be ta'en, let me be put to death;/ I am content, so thou wilt have it so." He welcomes death if that is Juliet's will. Hearing this, Juliet no longer feigns. It is the day, and he must leave. "It is the lark that sings so out of tune," she says. She makes the pun that the lark, supposed to make "sweet division" or lovely music, does not because she "divideth us." The bird's song is a sound like the hunter's "hunt's up" and pulls them apart, "arm from arm." It grows more and more light, she says. He must leave. Romeo replies that with more light, "more dark and dark our woes." Their night world, in which each gave light to the other, is over. Now the day world enters with the Nurse, who announces Lady Capulet is on her way to see Juliet, to tell her of her impending marriage to Paris. Juliet replies to the Nurse: "Then, window, let day in, and let life out." Romeo kisses Juliet and descends from the balcony on the rope ladder. Juliet's sense of the timelessness involved in their passion expresses itself:

> Art thou gone so? Love, lord, ay, husband, friend!
> I must hear from thee every day in the hour,
> For in a minute there are many days:
> O, by this count I shall be much in years
> Ere I again behold my Romeo!

To her question whether they shall ever meet again, Romeo comforts her with his assertion that in time to come they will find these travails "sweet discourses." But, suddenly, looking down at Romeo at the bottom of the ladder, Juliet has a terrible premonition — another one of Shakespeare's devices for underscoring the power of Fate.

> O God, I have an ill-divining soul!
> Methinks I see thee, now thou art below,
> As one dead in the bottom of a tomb;
> Either my eyesight fails, or thou look'st pale.

Romeo, newly transformed and strengthened by his wedding night, assures Juliet that she looks pale to him. It is "dry sorrow," or melancholy, that is making them pale and "drinking their blood." (The Elizabethans believed that such sorrow or melancholy consumed the blood and left the victim pale.) Romeo bravely bids her "adieu." Watching him leave, Juliet calls on fortune to be as fickle as men say that she is because then Romeo may soon return to her. When Lady Capulet finds Juliet a few moments later, she thinks Juliet's tears are for the dead Tybalt, little suspecting the irony of the situation — which the audience, alone, fully understands. She admonishes Juliet for too much weeping for the dead; some grief shows love but too much shows lack of it. Juliet and her mother immediately begin to talk on two levels. To her mother's remarks, Juliet always answers deceptively, referring to Romeo rather than Tybalt. The scene, therefore, develops its wordplay with something of the wit of high comedy. When Lady Capulet turns to Romeo as villain, Juliet's answers are again ambiguous. Juliet says that no man like

Irony

Romeo "doth grieve" her heart, and her mother answers: "That is, because the traitor murderer lives." "Ay, madam," says Juliet, "from the reach of these hands." She alone wants to revenge her cousin's death, but Lady Capulet, as fierce as always in her hatred of the Montagues, has already planned to have a hired assassin kill Romeo in Mantua. Juliet's answer to this horrifying news is that she would like to "temper" that poison (which her mother thinks means to increase the poison but which Juliet means to reduce) and she longs to wreak her revenge on the body of Romeo. The mother is pleased at Juliet's attitude and now will tell her "joyful tidings" which her "careful father," to put her "from thy heaviness," has planned for her. She is to marry the Count Paris next Thursday morning. Juliet immediately begins to weep and vows she will not marry Paris. She wonders at the haste; she has not even received Paris as a suitor. She will marry Romeo, Juliet says, before she will marry Paris. Old Capulet enters at this point, and Lady Capulet, as coldly as ever, turns her over to her father: "see how he will take it at your hands." Capulet first notices Juliet's tears. With a series of elaborate images, expressing, in their artificiality, his own bustling nature, he rebukes her tears and warns his beloved daughter the dangers of too much sorrow:

> In one little body
> Thou counterfeit'st a bark, a sea, a wind;
> For still thy eyes, which I may call the sea,
> Do ebb and flow with tears; the bark thy body is,
> Sailing in this salt flood; the winds, thy sighs;
> Who, raging with thy tears, and they with them,
> Without a sudden calm, will overset
> Thy tempest-tossed body.

His wife announces that Juliet refuses the offer of marriage, adding cruelly the curse "I would the fool were married to her grave," which ironically foreshadows the ending of the tragedy. The father cannot believe this refusal. He calls her proud, but Juliet answers with intricate wordplay that she can never be proud of what she hates, but thankful "even for hate, that is meant love." The use of paradox infuriates the old man. As with Tybalt, he will not brook insubordination from a minor. He ridicules her "chop-logic" or twisted logic of paradox. He becomes furious with her:

> Thank me no thankings, nor proud me no prouds,
> But fettle your fine points 'gainst Thursday next,
> To go with Paris to Saint Peter's Church,
> Or I will drag thee on a hurdle thither.

Lady Capulet tries to restrain the old man, and Juliet, kneeling, begs him to listen to her. He refuses and tells her that if she refuses to marry on next Thursday, he will disown her and throw her out of his house. She is not to speak, for the old man is ready to strike her: "my fingers itch."

She is their only child, he declares, and she is a curse to him and his wife. This is too much for the Nurse and she intervenes. Capulet quarrels back at her, but the Nurse holds her own even though he tells her to "utter your gravity o'er a gossip's bowl." Lady Capulet again tries to restrain him, but he is enraged beyond control. For years, says old Capulet, I have been arranging for a good match for you and now you refuse a splendid man. Capulet then mocks Juliet's voice in refusing. Finally, he lays down his injunction. Either she marries or she will be thrown out in the streets: "Graze where you will, you shall not house with me." He storms out, and Juliet is distraught. She loves her father and her family name, but her dilemma will not allow her to reveal her true reason. "Is there no pity," she cries out, "sitting in the clouds,/ That sees into the bottom of my grief?" Juliet turns to her mother for help, warning that if she refuses to help her, she will have a bridal bed in the funeral vault. Lady Capulet is at her coldest. She rejects her daughter completely: "Talk not to me, for I'll not speak a word:/ Do as thou wilt, for I have done with thee." On Lady Capulet's departure, Juliet in desperation turns to her oldest companion, her Nurse. "How shall this be prevented?" she asks. She cannot keep her faith in God and marry twice. Appealing for the last time to the Nurse, she begs for her to give her comfort and counsel. The power of Fate is too terrible for her: "Alack, alack, that heaven should practice strategems/ Upon so soft a subject as myself!" The Nurse's advice, far from comforting and helpful, is morally repelling, and for the first time reveals a horrible truth to Juliet: she is completely alone. The Nurse advises Juliet to have two marriages. Romeo is gone for good, or if he comes back, "it needs must be by stealth." She could marry Paris, "a lovely gentleman." In fact, Romeo is a dishcloth to him; the second marriage will be a happier one. In any case, "your first is dead; or 'twere as good he were,/ As living here and you no use of him." Juliet now knows that all of her world has rejected her — her father, her mother, and now the Nurse with her completely immoral suggestion — and that she is isolated as never before in her fourteen years. It is a terrible moment, and she still cannot believe the ugly words of her old Nurse. "Speak'st thou from thy heart?" she asks tenderly. "And from my soul too," says the lascivious old woman who has never understood the purity of the love for which she was the go-between. "Amen," says Juliet and before the Nurse can ask what she means, Juliet says ironically: "Well thou has comforted me marvelous much." She sends the old woman to tell her mother that she will go to Friar Laurence for confession because she has offended her father. But alone, Juliet expresses as frankly as ever her feelings. "Ancient damnation!" she calls the old woman. She remembers how many times the Nurse flattered Romeo and now condemns him and, worst of all, believes that Juliet herself could enter into such an immoral situation. "Thou and my bosom henceforth shall be twain," she says. She is completely isolated and if the Friar fails, she shall kill herself.

Commentary

The beginning of this scene offers another form of lyric verse, the *aubade* or traditional song sung at dawn. This song is one of the lyric heights of the tragedy, and its placidity contrasts with the furious fight which is soon to follow. Its serene liquid sound counterpoints the anguish of Juliet, completely isolated at the end of the scene. (Shakespeare is fond of such emotional contrasts in a single scene.) The lyric passage, or song, begins with the debate over the bird song: was it the lark or nightingale? The charm with which Juliet keeps Romeo back and his final surrender to her, only to have her bring him back to reality, is a result of the sophisticated banter over the bird's identity. In his first speech, Romeo expresses the appearance of the dawn in some of Shakespeare's loveliest lines, but what should be remembered is that the personification and metaphor are no longer exaggerated. Romeo's rhetoric has the ring of truth because the situation, the parting of the lovers after the bliss of their nuptial night, is poignant and ironic. Their night, their very bodies, are "burnt out." Ahead is what should be a "jocund" or joyful day, but they both know this may be their last night together. Romeo is strangely quiet in this scene, and the audience, remembering the Romeo in the Friar's cell, will wonder why. The answer is in the very peace of the lines (lines that reflect no violence, no sexual frustration, no fear). The great moment of joy has just passed, and after the communion of love, Romeo is deeply satisfied, deeply at peace with his nature and with his "stars." He has reached the deepest intensity of his passion, and the peace he feels is almost religious. It is Juliet who puns and, later in her premonition, shows the only traces of fear. Romeo shows the nobility of his nature in encouraging her in the midst of his own sorrow and farewell. Juliet's invocation to fortune is ironic, as the audience would recognize immediately. The fickleness of fortune would involve those very messages that Romeo promised to send.

The verbal banter which Lady Capulet provides is an excellent transition for Juliet to reach the most terrible moment of her life. Similarly, Capulet's rejection of Juliet had begun in jesting. His first speech about Juliet's tears had sounded like the jokes he made at the Capulet feast. His rhetorical conceit was a deliberate attempt to cheer his beloved daughter up. But suddenly she seems to turn against him. Because Juliet cannot give her reasons, he loses all understanding and violently rejects her. The coldness of her mother's final rejection is matched only by the vulgarity of the Nurse's reasons for her marriage to Paris. Her childhood is cut away from her more swiftly and violently than the loss of her girlhood during the wedding night just passed. What Shakespeare dramatized here is Juliet's womanly strength. She, like Romeo, never ceases to believe in the absolute nature of their love. Surrounded by all the realism of her family ties, of the social codes of Verona in which she is hardly more than an economic entity, and of the sexual amorality of the Nurse. Juliet never stops believing in the ideal truth and possibility of their love. She is finally ready to die for it at the end of the scene. With the previously attempted suicides of Romeo, and now Juliet's suicidal resolve, Shakespeare plants the deaths of the final act. It has never occurred to either one of them that each should not give all for their love, and it clearly never does.

ACT IV · SCENE 1

Summary

In Friar Laurence's cell, Paris asks the priest to bless his marriage on Thursday next. Friar Laurence is hesitant and complains about the speed. Old Capulet wants it that way, answers Paris. But you have not wooed the girl, rejoins the Friar. Paris gives, as his reason, Juliet's immoderate grief over Tybalt: "Venus smiles not in ·a house of tears." Further, Juliet's father is disturbed over her excessive melancholy and sees its dangers. Old Capulet believes, says Paris, marriage and new society would be a good cure. In an aside to himself, Friar Laurence longs to find a means to end the marriage. Suddenly Juliet enters. Paris immediately greets her: "Happily met, my lady and my wife!" Whatever Juliet's surprise at finding Paris where before she always found Romeo, she does not show it. Rather, she responds to Paris in dialogue which one might have found in Shakespeare's high comedy: stichomythic dialogue, or speeches of one line each that act as a kind of retort to the previous speech, a kind of repartee. The result is a swordplay, in a sense, of wits in which Juliet never betrays Romeo, but at the same time, never refuses Paris, as social propriety would demand. The wit thus helps Juliet to maintain her composure and to obey the social codes and manners of her society. Their light banter about her confession, her love for Friar Laurence, her tears, and her face are a dramatic rendering of her relationship to Paris, and a clear example of what her life in Verona might have been. But the moment Paris leaves, and Juliet is alone, she breaks forth with violent emotion. She is "past hope, past cure, past help!" If the Friar cannot give her advice, she will kill herself with "this knife." God united "my heart and Romeo's, thou our hands," and before she will dissolve her bond to Romeo, she will commit suicide. If his counsel does not help, the knife "shall play the umpire." His authority in that case will have had "no issue of true honor." Recognizing her desperate mood, Friar Laurence spies "a kind of hope." But she must have "strength of will" to "undertake/ A thing like death to chide away this shame." Juliet's answer is violent it its avowal to undertake anything to free herself of this marriage to Paris:

> O, bid me leap, rather than marry Paris,
> From off the battlements of yonder tower,
> Or walk in thievish ways; or bid me lurk
> Where serpents are; chain me with roaring bears;
> Or shut me nightly in a charnel house,
> O'ercovered quite with dead men's rattling bones,

66

With reeky shanks and yellow chapless skulls;
Or bid me go into a new-made grave
And hide me with a dead man in his shroud;
Things that, to hear them told, have made me tremble;
And I will do it without fear or doubt,
To live an unstained life to my sweet love.

Hearing this, Friar Laurence, who, as we saw in the first scene, is a scientist, draws forth a small bottle. He then reveals his plot. Juliet is to drink the vial in her bed the following night, and the effect will be that she will look dead: "no pulse/ Shall keep his native progress"; her face will have the pallor of death. For forty-two hours she shall continue in this state and then she shall awake as though from a pleasant sleep. In this way, Paris, who will come on the nuptial morning to receive her, will find her dead. "Then, as the manner of our country is," Juliet, supposedly dead, will lie on top of the bier and "be borne to that same ancient vault" of her family. In the meantime, Friar Laurence will convey a message to Romeo in Mantua, telling him the plot. When she awakes, therefore, Romeo and Friar Laurence will be there to take her away to Mantua. This plot, says Friar Laurence, will "free thee from this present shame." But it demands bravery and courage. Juliet cries out: "O, tell me not of fear!" He gives her the vial and prepares to send a message to Romeo by another friar. Juliet calls on "Love" to give her strength and hurries off.

Commentary

From the first, the audience had recognized the scientific and alchemical functions of Friar Laurence's character. The gathering of herbs in the earlier scene was a definite preparation for this climactic use of the drug for Juliet. The Friar's plot itself hinges, as does so much in the tragedy, on chance. Clearly the Friar should have gone to the feuding families and confessed the situation. But could he? Both Romeo and Juliet have promised suicide if their absolute love is in any way thwarted. Friar Laurence saw what such a confession before all of Verona might do to the private lovers. The plot therefore is a means of gaining time, and because it had to be devised rapidly, the element of chance is increased. It is Juliet's violence that finally convinces the priest what he must do in order to avert disaster. Once more, Juliet's resolve will take her through any kind of horror, even sleeping with a dead man on his shroud, if she can preserve the purity of her love. No Gothic terror is too much if she can avoid the real evil of betraying the ideal and absolute of her existence, the love she shares with Romeo. The hideous images in her speech would remind the audience of Juliet's violence of expression from the beginning. Shakespeare has carefully developed her character so that she, not Romeo, sees the dangers that threaten their isolated love and which she must bravely confront. It is interesting to note, too, that the whole of <u>Act IV is concerned with Juliet's act of courage,</u> a measure of her intensity of love.

ACT IV · SCENE 2

Summary

At the Capulet house, old Capulet is preparing for the wedding feast. He gives an invitation list to one servant and asks another for "twenty cunning cooks." The comic interchange between Capulet and the second servant provides a contrast to the previous scene and reveals the Elizabethan cordiality of the house. Turning to the Nurse, Capulet asks about Juliet. He hopes Friar Laurence will "do some good on her;/ A peevish self-willed harlotry it is." Juliet enters "with a merry look" and falls before her father, begging his pardon for "the sin/ Of disobedient opposition." Capulet is overjoyed and sends for Paris. He will advance the wedding date and have the wedding "tomorrow," or Wednesday. Juliet says that she met Paris at Friar Laurence's cell "and gave him what becomes love I might,/ Not stepping o'er the bounds of modesty." Capulet tells Juliet to rise, and in his joy he will go to visit Paris. Bustling as ever, the old man decides that "all our whole city is much bound" to Friar Laurence. When Juliet asks about new clothes for the wedding tomorrow, Lady Capulet says that tomorrow is too soon. But the old man will not agree. He will stay up the whole night preparing. "Let me alone," he says to Lady Capulet. "I'll play the housewife for this once." When all have left, he decides to tell Paris the news, for now "my heart is wonderous light." Juliet has obeyed his wishes and, thereby, shown him the love he had expected from her.

Commentary

The irony of this short scene lies in the contrast between the happy, active Capulet and the deception of Juliet. His bouncing egoism reveals the lord of a good English house and his ironic praise of Friar Laurence shows his complete failure to sense the impending tragedy. The speeding up of the wedding date is his own decision, and he cannot know he is the pawn of Fate. This is one more act of meaningless chance that the audience would feel could have been avoided. Juliet's love for Romeo can be measured again by the ease and success with which she deceives her father, mother, and Nurse. The deception itself is the clearest proof of her acceptance of her isolation.

ACT IV · SCENE 3

Summary

Juliet prepares to take the drug in her bedroom. After she and the Nurse have selected some clothes for the wedding, she lies to her old Nurse by asking her to leave so that she can pray. The Nurse especially, Juliet says in mock confidence, will understand that she should "move the heavens to smile upon my state,/ Which, well thou know'st, is cross and full of sin.'' Her mother enters, and Juliet is equally deceptive and bland in asking her to leave. She needs to rest. The Nurse can stay up with her mother all night in preparation for the morning's festivities. As the Friar had told her, she must be alone when she takes the drug, and so Juliet dismisses the others. But the moment her mother and the Nurse leave, Juliet drops her disguise and reveals the violence inherent in the situation. She may never see them again, and suddenly she is afraid.

> I have a faint cold fear thrills through my veins,
> That almost freezes up the heat of life:

She starts to call the Nurse back, but realizes sadly: ''My dismal scene I needs must act alone.'' Then Juliet picks up the vial and looks at it. Suppose, she thinks, the mixture does not work. Will she be married tomorrow? No, she says, putting the dagger on her bed, ''this shall forbid it.'' Her fears rise again when she thinks that perhaps the Friar has given her a poison so that he will not be dishonored by having married her and Romeo. ''I fear it is,'' she says. Yet she knows not, for the Friar has proven himself ''a holy man'' who has genuinely tried to help the lovers. Then deeper terrors enter her mind. If she should wake before Romeo arrives, would she ''be stifled in the vault''? If not stifled, perhaps the fear of the place and the night and all the bones of her ancestors, especially the presence of ''bloody Tybalt, yet but green in earth,'' will drive her insane. Spirits are said to walk abroad ''at some hours in the night.'' In an almost hypnotic state Juliet begins to recount the terrors that might confront her if she drinks the drug:

> Alack, alack, is it not like that I,
> So early waking, what with loathsome smells,
> And shrieks like mandrakes torn out of the earth,
> That living mortals, hearing them, run mad:—

Mandrakes or mandragora were narcotic and emetic roots that were supposed to grow from the bodies of executed criminals. They also took the shape of the human body because of their forked root. When torn from the earth, the mandrake roots were believed to utter terrible cries that drove the uprooter mad. The roots also had a sexual allusion. Shakespeare combines all three associations here to emphasize Juliet's feelings. In her violent emotional state, Juliet then imagines herself mad in the vault.

> Or, if I wake, shall I not be distraught,
> Environed with all these hideous fears,
> And madly play with my forefathers' joints,
> And pluck the mangled Tybalt from his shroud,
> And, in this rage, with some great kinsman's bone
> As with a club, dash out my desperate brains?

Finally, in a climax to her feelings, Juliet imagines that she now sees the ghost of Tybalt before her. This ultimate terror drives her to drink the potion. But it is in her final line that the audience learns that, for her love, Juliet will bravely dare to encounter any terror. She drinks to Romeo.

> O, look! Methinks I see my cousin's ghost
> Seeking out Romeo, that did spit his body
> Upon a rapier's point: stay, Tybalt, stay!
> Romeo, I come! This do I drink to thee.

Commentary

Juliet's soliloquy is one of the great achievements of language in the play. In it, Shakespeare has used the blank verse so flexibly that the emotional turbulence of Juliet's speech seems to reveal itself without any interruption by the form. The blank verse reinforces Juliet's terror and in no way restrains its fullest expression. The stacatto effect of the broken exclamations and comments is clearly balanced by the slow rise of terror which the steady iambic pentameter allows. The violence of the images has been prepared for during the entire tragedy, but especially in the strange calm of the previous scenes where Juliet has been required to deceive the world of her childhood. What Shakespeare is obviously trying to dramatize is that Juliet will face death in order to retain her love, the absolute of her existence. Such a dramatized fact is essential to make Juliet's suicide in the last act seem psychologically possible and genuinely motivated. But what also emerges from Juliet's brave confrontation of her own fearful imagining is the very depth of her love for Romeo. If she can still drink the potion, which may open up all these terrors, and have the full recognition of her possible death, then her love is stronger than her fear of death itself. To paraphrase, death is swallowed up in her love. The sacrifice of her own feelings seems to tell the audience that such an ideal love can command any sacrifice, even that of one's life. In this way the final suicides of both lovers are well planted in this scene. Already Juliet senses that Romeo exists in some eternity to which she must come when, although crazed with fear, she courageously drinks the potion. The isolation of their love finally is, at least in the lovers' mind, that of eternity.

ACT IV · SCENE 4

Summary

The Capulet household is all astir with preparations. It is the dawn of the day of the wedding of Juliet and Paris. The hurly-burly of the Nurse and Lady Capulet seeking provisions is heightened by the appearance of old Capulet, who calls all to "stir." It is already the time of the "curfew-bell" which was traditionally rung in early evening at eight or nine, but in Capulet's exaggeration, he means it is almost dawn, or "three o'clock." "Good Angelica" (the Nurse's ironic name) is to look after the baked meats and "spare not the cost." The tough old Nurse calls Capulet a "cot-quean" or man who foolishly busies himself in feminine activities and tells him to get to bed or he'll be sick during the day. Capulet replies that he has "watched" many a night for less cause. Lady Capulet, in the same good humor, says that he has been a "mouse-hunt" or woman-chaser in his time, but now she'll do the watching. Laughing them away, Capulet checks on the cooking, telling the servants to "make haste, make haste." He jokes with the second servant about drier logs. Then, the music of the Count Paris' retinue is heard. Juliet is to be awakened. The bridegroom has come.

Commentary

The irony of this short scene is again the contrast of lively bourgeois domestic details, and the haste involved, with the drugged Juliet (as the Elizabethan audience would know, just behind the curtain, in the inner stage). Capulet's household is clearly Elizabethan in its realism and in its lively humor. The humor of Capulet, his wife, and his servants would allow for the relief after Juliet's soliloquy and before the heavy laments of the next scene. Also, the haste will ironically emphasize the falsity of the whole proceeding.

ACT IV · SCENE 5

Summary

The Nurse enters Juliet's bedchamber and tries to wake her. She calls her affectionate names — "lamb," "slug-abed," "sweetheart," and finally "bride." She says Juliet is right to sleep now because tonight Paris will not let her sleep very much. When Juliet does not stir, she draws back the curtains of the bed and sees Juliet in her wedding clothes, seemingly asleep. Then she touches the young girl and realizes she is dead. Hearing the Nurse's cries, Lady Capulet enters and cries out to Juliet: "Revive, look up, or I will die with thee!" When Capulet enters, he will not believe that "she's dead," as Lady Capulet and the Nurse repeat over and over. Only when he touches Juliet, does he realize his daughter is dead. His fondness for extravagant expression finds the right and most touching image here for the extravagant spectacle of death:

> Life and these lips have long been separated:
> Death lies on her like an untimely frost
> Upon the sweetest flower of all the field.

The boisterous old man cannot speak, for Death, he says, has tied up his tongue. Friar Laurence and Paris enter with the musicians who were to accompany the bride to the church. Friar Laurence asks if the bride is ready. The vigorous Capulet finds his expression again and launches into a speech that carries one of the important images of the tragedy: the personification of Death as the lover and bridegroom. This image has been developed in some manner in the previous passages, but here it finds its fullest statement as, in the final scene of the tragedy, it will find its truest significance.

O son! The night before thy wedding day
Hath Death lain with thy wife. There she lies,
Flower as she was, deflowered by him.
Death is my son-in-law, Death is my heir;
My daughter he hath wedded: I will die,
And leave him all; life, living, all is Death's.

Paris is dismayed: he had longed for "this morning's face" but not for such a sight. Lady Capulet curses the day that has taken away her only child. The simple Nurse can merely repeat words: "O woeful day! O woeful day!" Paris, too, curses death and his misfortune. Capulet finishes his long passage of lament — which the Elizabethan audience would have accepted as a device of the Senecean tragedy popular in the theater of the 1590's — by cursing the untimeliness of Juliet's death. Suddenly Friar Laurence calls a halt to the laments. Of course, he alone — with the audience — knows the real truth, that Juliet only sleeps. He advises restraint. The cure for sorrow or "confusion" lies not in laments or "confusions." Through a kind of sophisticated logic, the Friar argues that heaven had a share in the young girl. Now heaven has all, and what her earthly parents could not prevent, i.e., her death, heaven does prevent through giving the girl immortal life. She is "advanced" to eternity, as they had always sought. This lamenting then is not true love for her. In a direct hint of Juliet's marriage to Romeo, the priest says: "She's not well married that lives married long;/ But she's best married that dies married young." Therefore, they should dry their tears and, as is the custom, stick the herb rosemary on the corpse. The body, again as is the custom, then should be borne, just as it is in wedding attire, to the vault of the Capulets. Nature, says the philosophic cleric, makes us weep, but reason laughs at such tears. Capulet then reverses all the festivities of the day, turning "our wedding cheer to a sad burial feast." The Friar enjoins all the mourners to go in and follow the body to the vault. He ends by pointing out that Providence is angry with them and that they should act quickly with Juliet's body and not offend that "high will." As the audience would understand, the Friar wants to make sure that his plot will work. The last part of this scene is a comic interlude that literally prepares the audience for the overwhelming tragedy of the last act. Peter, the Nurse's servant, asks the remaining musicians to play a favorite tune of his, "Heart's Ease." They ask him why. Because, says Peter, "my heart itself plays 'My heart is full of woe.'" When they refuse, he begins to teach them. It should be recalled that the great Elizabethan comic actor, Will Kempe, played this role and that, no doubt, the lines, as given here, are a mere pretext for his clowning. Peter quotes a famous Elizabethan song and asks a riddle from it, first to Simon Catling, then Hugh Rebeck, and finally James Soundpost. (These names were invented by Peter on the spot because a catling is a small lute string made of cat gut; a rebeck is the name of a three-stringed violin; and a soundpost is the peg on the inside of a stringed instrument.) None of them can answer the riddle. Peter does, with a laugh, and goes off, singing. The musicians scoff at him and then, because they are now mourners, they wait around and have dinner.

Commentary

It is ironical that this scene, given almost totally to lament, should be for someone who is not dead at all, and that the final suicides should have little or no formal mourning. The terrible events, set in motion by Romeo's touching of Juliet's hand at the Capulet ball, have now taken an irrefutable turn. They must lead to success or death. This is the only scene in the play in which neither of the lovers appear. It is for this reason a bit awkward, and the laments seem often as spurious as the sleeping figure of Juliet. Only Capulet, with his image of Death as the Lover — one of the great themes of European literature — gives the kind of relevance to the scene that it truly requires. He will be, of course, more true than he knows, and the dramatic irony here relies on the audience's awareness of the last scene. The rather stark and generally undifferentiated laments and the dramatic reversal of wedding to funeral are lightened by the antics of the clown Peter. But the joke is obviously more than the printed lines, and it, too, seems awkward at this moment. The forces of Fate are moving with too much of the dreadful speed which Romeo and Juliet have set in motion with their love.

ACT V · SCENE 1

Summary

In Mantua, Romeo, awaiting news from Verona, relates a happy dream he has just had. He has dreamed that he was dead and Juliet woke him with a kiss, and then he "revived and was an emperor." How sweet is love itself when its shadows are "so rich in joy," he says. Balthasar enters and when Romeo asks how Juliet fares, he answers she is well because her body sleeps in the Capulet vault and "her immortal part with angels lives." Romeo's answer is simple and direct in its sorrow (unlike the laments of the last scene): "Is it even so? Then I defy you stars!" Immediately Romeo prepares to leave for Verona. Balthasar, seeing his face, beseeches him to have "patience": "Your looks are pale and wild, and do import/ Some misadventure." Romeo says he is deceived, and then asks Balthasar: "Hast thou no letters to me from the friar?" When the audience would hear the answer of "no," it would immediately recognize another one of those accidents of chance that seem to dominate the play. Balthasar leaves to get the horses, and Romeo, left alone, utters the words that would tell the audience of his intentions: "Well, Juliet, I will lie with thee tonight." Seeking the means to accomplish his suicide, he remembers an apothecary nearby whose personal appearance and whose shop showed immense poverty. Such a poor man would sell him poison, although the law of Mantua forbids such sale. When the poor apothecary emerges, Romeo hands him forty gold coins and asks for "a dram of poison, such soon-speeding gear/ As will disperse itself through all the veins." He seeks the means of sudden death, "as violently as hasty powder fired/ Doth hurry from the fatal cannon's womb." When the apothecary objects, Romeo reminds the man of his poverty and tells him that "the world is not thy friend nor the world's law." The man agrees, and after he has received the poison, Romeo gives him the gold, calling it "worse poison to men's souls." Leaving, Romeo calls the poison a "cordial" or medicine for the heart. It will go with him to Juliet's grave, "for there must I use thee."

Commentary

The central purpose of this scene is to reveal Romeo's reaction to Juliet's presumed death and Romeo's plot to kill himself. It begins ironically. As in many instances throughout the play, another premonition of the final scene occurs. Romeo has dreamed that he is dead (a fact that he quickly dismisses, but which the Elizabethan audience would perceive immediately as important). Juliet's kisses bring him to life, and he wakes up with great joy. This kind of emotional state is a device that dramatists through the ages have used. The moment of greatest joy precedes the moment of greatest fall. When he learns of Juliet's burial, explained by Balthasar in the same terms as the Friar in the previous scene (she is more alive in heaven than on earth), Romeo's reaction is simple and direct. He defies the stars. The stars have functioned in two ways in the play: (1) as representing the lovers to each other in their light/ darkness imagery and therefore as a kind of free will for each other; and (2) as symbolizing the forces of Fate working on the lovers. Here Romeo refers to this second function. He will not accept his "star-crossed" destiny of living without Juliet. His simple reaction is proof of the transformed Romeo. If the audience would recall the Romeo of the first scenes, or even the Romeo of the Friar's cell, it would see immediately the difference. Love has transformed him. Like Juliet with her "poison," he too will nobly undertake any sacrifice to retain the absolute of his existence, his love for Juliet. In Mantua, all Romeo can do is to dream of his love. This action is not unlike the idealist-lover of the first scenes, but it is no longer rhetoric, it is fact and action. The proof of this state is his immediate plot. He will seek poison. The long description of the apothecary and his shop may seem irrelevant at this point in the swift action. But the description and the ensuing dialogue has this meaning: Romeo and Juliet are now reduced, as outcasts from society, to this kind of underworld. Had they lived, this kind of mean existence might have been theirs. The world had not been the apothecary's friend; the world has not been Romeo's nor Juliet's. Further, the transformed Romeo has a universal sympathy, born of his love and sorrow, for all creatures. Finally, a key line in the scene is Romeo's when he first announces his plot. He will "lie" with Juliet that night. He means, of course, that he will kill himself beside her, but also Romeo uses the pun of "lie" as meaning sexual intercourse and behind it all is the grim irony of "dying" as both physical expiration and sexual intercourse. It is another version of the theme of Death and marriage, of love-in-death, that climaxes in the last act.

ACT V · SCENE 2

Summary

Friar Laurence, in his cell, welcomes a brother friar, Friar John, who had taken a letter to Romeo in Mantua. Friar John's story is one of accident. Before he left Verona for Mantua, he stopped to find another "barefoot brother," or Franciscan, to go with him. But the other brother was visiting the sick. While Friar John was explaining what he wanted, the "searchers of the city," who sought out cases of plague, found them in a house they suspected of plague, and sealed both friars up until today. To Friar Laurence's question about the letter, Friar John answers that no one would deliver it for fear of infection. Friar Laurence bewails the force of accident, but immediately tells Friar John to bring a crowbar (with which to force the vault). Juliet will awaken in three hours and will censure him for not having Romeo there. He will, however, keep her in his cell until Romeo will arrive. He ends the scene by setting the mood of the next scene: "Poor living corpse, closed in a dead man's tomb".

Commentary

Friar Laurence's exclamation is the key to this scene as it is to the whole series of events in the last two acts. The very rush with which Friar Laurence ends the short scene will increase the melodramatic suspense in the audience's mind. Friar Laurence cannot know, as the audience does, that Romeo's life is literally at stake and dependent on the Friar's speed in arriving at the tomb. Romeo had asked twice in the last scene for letters from Friar Laurence. Now the audience learns why these letters never came. If the events seem too accidental, one should remember that in action or plot so quickly paced and so timed that nothing can go wrong, the least miscalculation or accident can throw the whole chain of events off. The speed of the play, with which this scene ends, is the real force that causes the accidents, and the speed results as much from character as from exterior forces. Free will and fate blend together in working out the plan of Providence, Shakespeare seems to be saying. Accident is an outcome of the speed of the various plots, themselves the effect of each character's desires. In either case, Providence is manipulating character and accident for its own ends.

ACT V · SCENE 3

Summary

The final scene of the tragedy opens in the churchyard of the Capulet vault late at night. Paris appears with his page. He instructs the page to wait "under yond yew trees" and hold his ear to the ground, loose from the digging of many graves, to hear anyone approaching. The page is to whistle if anyone does approach. Paris takes some flowers from the page, who, leaving, remarks to himself how afraid he is of the churchyard. Paris then strews the flowers on the outside of Juliet's vault:

> Sweet flower, with flowers thy bridal bed I strew —
> O woe! Thy canopy is dust and stones —
> Which with sweet water nightly I will dew,
> Or, wanting that, with tears distilled by moans:
> The obsequies that I for thee will keep
> Nightly shall be to strew thy grave and weep.

Suddenly, Paris hears the boy's whistle. He curses the intruder that has come "to cross my obsequies and true love's rite." He hides himself as Romeo and Balthasar enter with a torch and instruments with which to open Juliet's vault. Romeo takes the crowbar and mattock from Balthasar and gives him the letter which he had intended to write two scenes earlier. It is a letter to his parents telling them of the reasons for his death. He takes the torch from Balthasar and fiercely admonishes him not to follow him into the vault. Romeo lies and pretends that he is entering the vault to see Juliet's face and to take a ring from her. Again, he warns Balthasar that if he should be suspicious and try to return, Romeo

> will tear thee joint by joint
> And strew this hungry churchyard with thy limbs:
> The time and my intents are savage-wild,
> More fierce and more inexorable far
> Than empty tigers or the roaring sea.

Balthasar agrees, and Romeo, handing him a purse of gold, bids him farewell: "Live, and be prosperous." Again, Romeo's warm farewell reveals his new-found sympathy for all creatures. Balthasar, in an aside, knows that something terrible is about to happen and instead of leaving, he hides in the churchyard. Romeo turns to force open the vault, or tomb, of Juliet. The metaphor he uses is a powerful and violent one, suited to his mood of hate. He will revenge himself on death by forcing open its mouth, or the tomb, and in cramming it with more food, or himself. The word "womb" recalls the sexual imagery of the tragedy. In the death-marriage, now about to be consummated in the tomb, Romeo for the last time will enter the "womb of death" and climax his love by "dying" (as explained previously, an Elizabethan euphemism for sexual intercourse as well as Romeo's suicide). In entering the tomb, violently tearing it open with his tools, he literally rapes Death. He literally fornicates with Death and crams it with more food. The suicides of the lovers will be, therefore, the Death-marriage. The two opening apostrophes (or figures of speech which are forms of direct address) emphasize the violence of his defiance of Death:

> Thou detestable maw, thou womb of death,
> Gorged with the dearest morsel of the earth,
> Thus I enforce thy rotten jaws to open,
> And in despite, I'll cram thee with more food!

Paris hears only the hatred of this speech. He assumes that Romeo is there to do damage to the Capulet vault in which Tybalt lies, and, as a result of whose death, Juliet died of grief. He steps forth and tells Romeo to stop "thy unhallowed toil." "Can vengeance be pursued further than death?" he asks. "Thou must die." Romeo answers: "I must indeed; and therefore came I hither." He begs Paris, a "good gentle youth," not to tempt a "desperate man." Romeo recognizes his condition as the final madness of melancholy, and he begs Paris not to cause him to put "another sin upon my head,/ By urging me to fury." Leave me, he cries, and say "a madman's mercy bade thee run away." But Paris will not leave, and Romeo is provoked. They fight, and the page runs out to call the watch. Paris is slain. His last wish is that he be placed beside Juliet. Romeo agrees. Yet, only when he kneels and looks at the face of the youth, does he recognize him as Paris, Mercutio's kinsman. He then recalls what in his melancholy he had only half-heard. Paris was to have wed Juliet. Romeo takes Paris' hand in another gesture of universal sympathy. They are brothers in their death for love. Paris is also "one writ with me in sour misfortune's book," using the same image for Paris that Lady Capulet had used when first describing him. Romeo will bury Paris in more than a "triumphant grave." He will have a lighthouse to mark his grave because "here lies Juliet, and her beauty makes/ This vault a feasting presence full of light." This last reference to the light/ darkness imagery would be accented before the audience's eyes by the single torch held by Romeo in the darkness of the vault. Romeo then speaks to Death familiarly and tells him to lie beside Paris. After this speech, Romeo brings Paris' body into the vault. He notes his own state of excitement, almost gaiety, and it recalls a punning image of lightning — the image of light and explosion that Juliet had mentioned in the balcony scene and which, as some critics have noted, is the very essence of the tragedy.

> How oft when men are at the point of death
> Have they been merry! Which their keepers call
> A lightning before death: O, how may I
> Call this a lightning?

Now Romeo moves to the bier where Juliet lies in her wedding dress. He can barely speak: "O my love! My wife!" Personifying death again, Romeo notices how Juliet still looks alive (a dramatic irony, of course, since she is in fact alive).

> Death, that hath sucked the honey of thy breath,
> Hath had no power yet upon thy beauty:
> Thou are not conquered; beauty's ensign yet

Is crimson in thy lips and in thy cheeks,
And death's pale flag is not advanced there.

Looking at Tybalt's corpse, Romeo says that he will give the man whom he killed the favor of seeing his death and in another act of sympathy, asks Tybalt's forgiveness. He looks at Juliet and cannot understand how she can still be beautiful. Then, climaxing Death as the lover there, he says:

Shall I believe
That unsubstantial death is amorous,
And that the lean abhorred monster keeps
Thee here in dark to be his paramour?

To prevent that, says Romeo in an extravagant conceit, I'll never leave "this place of dim night" and "remain/ With worms that are thy chambermaids." In the tomb he will "set up my everlasting rest/ And shake the yoke of inauspicious stars/ From this world-wearied flesh." With the reference to stars, the audience recognizes that the force of Fate has come full circle. Romeo prepares to kill himself. "Eyes" are to look their last. "Arms" are to take their "last embrace" and "lips" that are "the doors of breath" are to kiss Juliet, to "seal with a righteous kiss/ A dateless bargain to engrossing death!" He takes the vial from his pocket and addresses a series of apostrophes to it:

Come, bitter conduct, come, unsavory guide!
Thou desperate pilot, now at once run on
The dashing rocks thy seasick weary bark!

Thus, at the height of melancholy and despair, he drains the vial: "O true apothecary!" Romeo dies, kissing Juliet. At the other end of the churchyard, Friar Laurence enters, crying "Saint Francis be my speed!" Balthasar greets him and tells him that the torch they see in the Capulet vault is Romeo's. The Friar hurries on but Balthasar will not enter as he was commanded. The Friar is full of premonitions and fears "some ill unlucky thing." Balthasar has dreamed — what in fact he half-heard — that Romeo has killed someone. When the Friar, moving on, finds the blood and "gory swords" and then the body of Paris, he cries out: "Ah, what an unkind hour/ Is guilty of this lamentable chance!" It is the force of accident again. At this moment Juliet begins to stir from her drugged sleep. She asks the Friar for Romeo. Before he can answer, the sound of approaching townsmen is heard. "A greater power than we can contradict/ Hath thwarted our intents," says the Friar, and points to the dead Romeo and Paris. He will now take Juliet and dispose of her "among a sisterhood of holy nuns." But she delays, and in these moments the whole impact of the tragedy strikes her. Finally, the Friar feels he can no longer stay for his own safety. Juliet tells him to leave. She will not go. He leaves and Juliet opens Romeo's hand and finds the vial. "O churl!" she says, with a kind of wit ("churl" being the equivalent to "bad boy"), "drunk all, and left no friendly drop/ To help me after?" She kisses

Romeo, hoping some poison still remains on his lips. She finds them still warm, and as the watch is heard approaching, she takes out his dagger. She thrusts it into her body, saying, in a final conceit, that her body is the sheath of the dagger. "There rust," she says, "and let me die." She too follows her lover into what she believes is the absolute of their love. She dies as the page leads the watchmen into the vault. There, they find the corpses, and several men are sent to tell the Prince and the two families. Others search the grounds and find Balthasar and then Friar Laurence, "that trembles, sighs, and weeps." Thus far, however, "the true ground of all these piteous woes" is not clear. Soon the Prince enters — dramatic time is often capsuled, as here — and with him the Capulets. What has broken the dawn sleep of the citizens of Verona? the Prince asks. Then they all see the suicides. Capulet cannot understand how Juliet's dagger is from the sheath of a Montague. Lady Capulet feels that the sight has warned her old age "to a sepulchre." Montague enters, and the Prince greets him with wordplay: "thou art early up,/ To see thy son and heir more early down." Montague announces that his wife has died the previous night from grief over Romeo's exile, but at the sight of his son, he rebukes the corpse: "O thou untaught! What manners is this,/ To press before thy father to a grave?" The Prince then commands all to be silent and the churchyard to be sealed off until the facts of the case can be ascertained. Friar Laurence steps forward, and proceeds to "impeach and purge/ Myself condemned and myself excused." He then tells the story of the lovers and the various plots and the accidents of chance, not forgetting to blame himself:

> and, if aught in this
> Miscarried by my fault, let my old life
> Be sacrificed, some hour before his time,
> Unto the rigor of severest law.

The Prince forgives him for his part in the crime: "We still have known thee for a holy man." Balthasar then tells his story and gives the letter to the Prince. Paris' page confirms the purpose of his master's visit. Romeo's letter proves the Friar's story and his own purpose in coming to the vault. The Prince, after this recital of facts, decides that the real villains are those who have kept up the feud which has finally destroyed the heirs of both warring families. This indictment includes himself for not taking firmer measures with the families. As a result, he has lost two kinsmen, Paris and Mercutio.

> Where be these enemies? Capulet! Montague!
> See, what a scourge is laid upon your hate,
> That heaven finds means to kill your joys with love.
> And I for winking at your discords too
> Have lost a brace of kinsmen: all are punished.

The families agree that Providence found "means" to heal their hate. Romeo and Juliet are martyrs, or as Montague says, "poor sacrifices of our enmity!" Like saints or heroes, Romeo and Juliet will be given statues of pure gold that will remind all of Verona of the merit of two martyrs. The religious imagery that introduced the two lovers is here come full circle. Their love finally served a religious purpose, healing the society of Verona. Their love was greater than the hate of the world that had isolated them. The Prince ends the tragedy. The sun will not shine today "for sorrow." The two families must talk more, and "some shall be pardoned, and some punished." Above all, he says, the tragedy of the waste of these lovers must be felt.

> For never was a story of more woe
> Than this of Juliet and her Romeo.

Commentary

Another form of lyric verse to be found in the play is the *elegy*, or poem commemorating a dead person. Paris' speech before the Capulet tomb is an example of elegy. It is unusual, when the scene opens, to find Paris and not the many characters who have all been rushing to Juliet's tomb. For this scene is the culmination of the drama. What has been promised in the Prologue — the death of "star-crossed" lovers — will be here fulfilled. It is, therefore, odd to find Paris dominating the first part of the scene. Yet his idealistic love for Juliet parallels Romeo's and it is fitting that Romeo later calls him brother as, when he does not recognize Paris, Romeo also calls him a youth (although the man before Romeo is his same age). Love has matured Romeo more than Paris, and has given him universal sympathies and the feeling of wisdom and age. But had he lived, Paris would have come every night, like the true courtly lover, to wash the dust from the tomb with his tears. One of the ironies that keeps repeating in the tragedy is that men die without knowing the full consequence of their acts. Here, Paris cannot know that Romeo is married to Juliet.

The quiet violence that the audience had noted in the first scene of Act Five is here developed. In telling Balthasar to leave, Romeo says that the situation and his own mood are "savage-wild" and more fierce than "empty tigers or the roaring sea." His fierce defiance continues in the famous mouth metaphor for death and then in the suddenness and fury with which Romeo destroys Paris. He feels the exhilaration of his state and sees it as lightning, one of the great image patterns of the play. His playing with Death personified emphasizes this violence; and as he obviously recognizes, he is mad with melancholy just as his friends and family had predicted he might be. The rhetoric of his death speech is also touching in its despair and melancholy. The dramatic strategy has brought him to this moment with a terrible logic, and this same logic demands adequate expression. The force of the moment he clearly places in "the yoke of inauspicious stars" on his "world-wearied flesh." Fate has ruled against him, he thinks, and he is tired, in despair. But his final kiss promises "a dateless bargain" and the gallant toast of the vial to "my love" reminds the audience that he sees his love as eternal. As Juliet, when she earlier drank her vial, so he, too, sees their absolute and ideal love existing, above his own weakness and melancholy, in the realm of eternity. He is willing to sacrifice for his absolute idealism of love, as found in the intense and concrete reality of his passion for Juliet and hers for him. He dies with a kiss, never ceasing for one moment to believe in the eternity of his passion. The effect of preparation for this scene and, especially, the magic of the words themselves convince the audience of his belief. The center of the scene is his death and Juliet's. Juliet really says little, but her great confrontation with death was in an earlier scene. At that time, she had triumphed over her fears in her sacrifice for Romeo. Now, violently stabbing herself with the dagger, she merely fulfills what Shakespeare, in consummate dramatic construction, had prepared in her character from the balcony scene to this point. To the end she retains her wit, rebuking Romeo for having left her "no friendly drop" and finally kissing him with the hope of finding poison there which will act as "a restorative." To both lovers, therefore, there seems no doubt but their love will not only exist in eternity, but will find its freedom there.

Shakespeare usually ends his tragedies with some element of order reconciling the chaos caused by the tragic events of the play. Critics have often complained about this final scene in which the action of the drama is laboriously retold. But the Elizabethan audience would see the necessity for such a scene. The Prince, who represents justice and order in the society of Verona, must learn the facts before making a judgment. Psychologically, the audience needs a moment to let its mind dwell on the meaning of the blood-strewn bodies before it. It needs an obituary calm in which the accounts can be tabulated, and proven, before the feuding families — and the Prince himself — can recognize their guilt. In other words, the scene of private love (and suicide) needs a social dimension before it can be public tragedy. The scene is brilliantly constructed so that there is always rising action and suspense despite the awareness of an obvious conclusion (which the Prologue had told the audience). But "the fearful passage of their death-marked love" must have direction to contemplate that conclusion. The Elizabethan audience was not interested in the intensity of private love, whatever its beauty of expression. Tragedy demanded a greater range. The calm at the end of the play therefore provides that range. The audience could see that Fate has intervened to carry out the demands of Providence. The society of Verona has been united once more through the sacrificial deaths of the young lovers. The gold statues that will commemorate them represent society's awareness of their redemptive act. The final lines invite the audience to contemplate the waste of the tragedy — and by implication, the intensity of its formal expression — and the sense of guilt that all share who have participated in the tragedy.

Structure
Methods Of Analyzing Structure

A writer works like a carpenter. He joins section to section to form a whole. Of course, his idea of what the whole will look like will vary in its depth from the carpenter's idea of the whole. But the essential process of making is similar enough. All works of literature are formed in just such prosaic labor with things. The materials for the workshop of the literary artist are naturally the materials of daily life as viewed by all of us, but it is the writer's intensity of experience that enables him to see more deeply than most of us into the "skull beneath the skin," as T.S. Eliot once said. That is, the writer penetrates (often whether he wants to or not, such are the demands of talent or genius) through the usual surface of realistic daily life and takes the materials and forms them in his own workshop. He makes these materials into something. This making of materials is structure, and, in a larger sense, form. Now it should be said immediately that structure is as variable and as significant as the individual writer's interest, personality, and talent. *King Oedipus* and *Death of a Salesman* are fortunately two different works. As Henry James once commented about his own literary art, the House of Fiction has many windows. There are, therefore, as many forms and structures to be found in literary organisms as a zoologist or botanist might find in the natural world.

The purpose of this brief discussion is to offer the student some possible means of ascertaining the reality of structure both in *Romeo and Juliet* and in any other literary work. But, like all evidences of organic life, structure cannot be taught so much as discovered. In the process of discovery, the student will probably ask himself three questions, which will function as devices for discovering the structure of a literary work:

1. Why do I see this work as a whole?
2. Why do I see this work in parts?
3. Why do I see this work as an idea?

The student will be lucky if he can even *approximate* answers to these three questions. But he must try if he is to understand the mysterious action of structure in any literary work. Strengthened by such discoveries, he can then turn to specific questions about the structure of *Romeo and Juliet* with some degree of assurance. In no case will the answers be final, either to the larger questions about literary structure or to the more specific queries about *Romeo and Juliet*. This is not to say that their truth is relative. The nature of a literary work involves absolute truth like every other organism in the universe. But our perception of this absolute truth in literature grows as we live. Literature is not mathematics or the science of the computer. On the contrary, great works of literature, like *Romeo and Juliet*, demand patience and contemplation and "silence" if their forms are to reveal itself. Their answers are not automatic. But let us first see how these three questions about structure can possibly begin the process of discovery.

1. Why do I see this work as a whole?

A good student will abandon himself to the important work of literature. That is, he will let the author ask the questions, answer them, relate them, and resolve them. Clearly this is Coleridge's "willing suspension of disbelief." Often, in having a work assigned, the student will feel obligated, usually because he is pressed by time, to work piecemeal, feeling that he is lost without grabbing at the parts on a first (and probably only) reading. But usually with an important work, like *Romeo and Juliet*, he cannot help being drawn into the excitement of the whole action. How does this effect of the whole occur? Primarily, through plot. Therefore, the first place to start in analyzing structure is the plot. Aristotle stated long ago that the soul of tragedy is plot. Such is especially true in Shakespearean drama, and nowhere truer than in *Romeo and Juliet*. Aristotle also commented that tragedy (or the work of literature) was an imitation of an action that was "complete, whole, and of a certain magnitude." A plot, continued Aristotle, provides this sense of the whole. The whole, he explained, arose through the functioning of a beginning, middle, and end, and he demonstrated such unity of plot from the works of his own day.

The Victorian critic, A.C. Bradley, in his famous lectures on Shakespearean tragedy, has shown how this same sense of the plot as the whole operates in Shakespeare. The whole in Shakespearean tragedy is divided into three movements which, naturally, overlap and mingle: the Exposition; the Conflict; and the Catastrophe. The Exposition, as Bradley demonstrates, comprises most of the dramatic action of the First Act. Like all dramas, the plot of a Shakespearean tragedy demands background information. The audience must get introduced to the little world of the characters. It must know their hates and loves as well as their social and economic levels. Above all, the audience must know the situation out of which the Conflict or the next stage of the plot will arise. The Exposition must introduce us to the leading characters and show us how naturally they will act and react in the pressures of the Conflict and Catastrophe. The moment the audience has this introduction, the Exposition ceases.

In *Romeo and Juliet* the Exposition is complete when Romeo and Juliet meet at the Capulet feast. The whole of Act I has led to this encounter, and now all the necessary information is given. Shakespeare has skillfully begun his narrative with a short public scene in which the truth of what the prologue has told the audience — that is, the feud of the Montagues and Capulets — is dramatized to the audience through the excitement and violence of a street battle. Then, relaxing his grasp, Shakespeare has given the audience key information about first Romeo and then Juliet. Finally, just before their encounter, Romeo has a premonition of his future death. The encounter is the logical climax of such a narrative development of Exposition.

The Conflict, which begins with the meeting of the two lovers, will emphasize the struggle inherent in the basic materials of the story. Here, the Conflict will be based on the feud of the Montagues and Capulets and will be revealed in the varying fortunes of the two lovers, their love in conflict with its social and fatal consequences. Therefore, there will be in the Conflict, as Bradley points out, "ups and downs" in the dramatic action, a "sustained alternation" between reversals and successes in the tragedy, often, as in *Romeo and Juliet*, in startlingly ironic patterns. The irony and this sense of rising and falling in the dramatic tension add to our sense of narrative and therefore to our sense of the whole. Finally, the Catastrophe ends the sense of the dramatic action "complete, whole, and of a certain magnitude." The death of the lovers, their final encounter, is the key to the whole movement of form in *Romeo and Juliet*. The action cannot go beyond that. Thus, the student who has abandoned himself (and his sense of time) to the whole of the work, to a "willing suspension of disbelief," will find himself rewarded by a sense of the whole which the plot is most instrumental in achieving. Consequently, the student should familiarize himself with the logical development of the plot. First he should determine the order of events before the explanation of events. Knowledge of the plot in all its intricate changes is the best way to begin to understand the whole effect of literary structure.

2. Why do I see this work in parts?

When he has surveyed the whole, the student will naturally turn to the elements that make up the plot. What are the links between these elements? Further, how do these parts function in relationship to the whole? Or, how are these parts directed in themselves toward crucial points of dramatic tension? For example, how is the speech of Friar Laurence to Romeo in the Second Act really directed toward the final catastrophe? These are some of the questions that the student will want to ask himself as he surveys the parts of the logical whole that any good literary work should be. These last queries especially lead to the question of preparation in a tragedy.

Shakespeare was a master of the element of structure. In *Romeo and Juliet*, especially, Shakespeare "plants" key concepts, key actions, even key phrases and images that will blossom into important thematic patterns as the drama develops. He thus takes each part and builds, like a true craftsman, toward the crucial scenes. The narrative, as in *Romeo and Juliet*, often uses accident and chance to increase the sense of preparation, but the most effective means of preparation is clearly Shakespeare's handling of character in individual scenes. In these parts or scenes, the character reveals his motives, often mere responses to the force of the plot but more likely his own freedom of action and choice within the dramatic conflict of the plot. Yet the intimate relationship between character and plot cannot be so easily arranged. Character is quite literally plot; and the character's individual motives, or "plots," form the preparatory links that unite the parts of any fictional whole. As Heraclitus pointed out long ago, "a man's character is his fate." To understand the individual parts of the whole plot is to understand, in a real manner, the meaning of character as it prepares for crucial scenes or relates its part to the whole through dramatic action.

A.C. Bradley is helpful here, too. For the parts of a plot, especially in a Shakespearean tragedy, follow a certain pattern in relating to the whole tragedy and to each other. The First Act is usually the time of preparation, the real conflict still underground, as it were. The Second Act begins the various levels of the conflict, with the slow movement of Force A against the dominant power of Force B in a series of carefully modulated movements of success and failure. The Third Act almost always embodies the crucial scene of the drama, the turning point, after which the action is irrevocable in its movement toward the catastrophe. Now the fortunes of Force A are at their height and simultaneously declining. In Act Four, therefore, there is a slow decline of Force A and a rise in the fortunes of Force B (or its transformed equivalent). In Act Five the catastrophe results, in which Force A is usually physically destroyed but spiritually triumphant. The difficult moments in the drama therefore — at least if the parts are to relate to the whole — are the moments in the Third Act and in the Fourth Act. In the Third Act the crucial action must be truly a turning point, a dramatic action that really shapes the action toward the catastrophe. In the Fourth Act, the problem is a sustaining of interest in the parts or scenes, as the fated hero (and heroine) move toward their inevitable end. Shakespeare is especially ingenious in his treatment of the Fourth Act. In *Romeo and Juliet*, for example, the fortunes of the lovers have definitely declined from the Third Act. Thus, Romeo is not present through the entire Fourth Act. What we see is the plot of Juliet to escape her parents' wish for her to marry Paris. In fact, we do not see Juliet for two scenes except as drugged and asleep. Consequently, Shakespeare ingeniously delays the catastrophe but sustains the interest.

Bradley's analysis of the parts of a tragedy are applicable, quite obviously, *mutatis mutandis,* to any serious work of literature. Even a picaresque novel like *Catcher in the Rye* has the rudiments of such analysis, ultimately derived like all such analyses from Aristotle's concept of the beginning, middle, and end. In such a novel, there is an introduction to the main character, to the dilemma before him, and to the very style through which this dilemma will be filtered. In this way, the various conflicts are introduced and slowly developed into the area of complication, with episode after episode revealing the rising action. Finally a period of crisis arrives, a crucial moment in which an action must be chosen. After that choice, or climax of the previous action, the hero is irrevocably committed to a course of action (or a level of perception which will, in turn, precipitate that action). Thus the remainder of the work is falling action or "unknotting" or denouement, leading inevitably to the catastrophe at the end, whatever form that catastrophe may take. (Of course, unlike the Shakespearean tragedy, the physical death of the hero is not always demanded.) The point in all such analysis is to see how the variously inter-relating parts operate in themselves and in their function as preparation for the key scenes or key parts which must give us that sense of the unity of the plot or, in Aristotle's phrase, of the work of literature as being "complete, whole, and of a certain magnitude."

3. Why do I see this work as an idea?

This question is the most difficult of all to answer because the answer is one of perception, the individual student's perception. To see the work of literature finally as a complete entity is to see, of course, the "idea" or complete organism of the work. It lies in that area of perception which is called "aesthetic unity." The parts can be viewed now, after analysis, as genuine elements of the whole. It is clear, for example, why the Nurse in her first long speech, mentions her daughter Susan and especially the sexual joke about Juliet which her husband had made years before. The very power of the final scene in the Capulet tomb depends on just such a series of perceptions on the student's part. Now they all add up. Now the parts are elements of a whole. But something is different about this whole, or unity. It is not that dazzling first sight that the plot so brilliantly gives. It is more like the seeing of motion before one's eyes, the mysterious movement of a living organism. The entire literary work vibrates with its own peculiar life, its own *idea* of itself in which no part is separate but every part is a whole in itself and yet participates in the whole structure *at the same time*. Finally, the point of judgment of the success or failure of the whole (and of the parts as each contributes to that whole) has come. The student must ask himself the crucial question if the work as an "idea" survives. If his answer is "yes," he will discover a unique phenomenon found in all great organisms. This is that the individual parts, marvelous in themselves, are added up into a sum or whole that is greater than the number of the parts. That is, the final effect of a Shakespearean tragedy, or any good literary work, is that of a unity or whole that cannot be explained by the simple combination of its parts. The whole, the aesthetic or organic unity, is what moves us emotionally and on every level of our being (as the work is in degree good or bad). The result of this final effect is that the student will not merely contemplate the work of art as parts formed into a whole. He will *participate* in the work. He will belong to its whole himself. Its life will somehow become his, and the student will be a different person. Quite simply, he has received a new "idea." As the German poet Rainer Maria Rilke once wrote, the effect of art is always a command: "You must change."

Questions and Answers on the Structure
of *Romeo and Juliet*

Question 1.

What is the central action of *Romeo and Juliet* and how does the structure of the play reveal the development of this action?

Answer

The central action of *Romeo and Juliet* is the love of the two young people. It is never allowed to decline within itself once the lovers have met each other in the First Act and made their sonnet-encounter. Neither ceases to believe in the absolute nature of their passion. Unlike Shakespeare's great tragedies, there is no movement within the lovers themselves, no inner meditation, that is, about the moral probity of their passion. Both are willing to go to any limits, from the simplest scaling of a wall or a balcony to the agonies of drugs and deception and finally to the outer limits of life itself through a suicide pact. The central action of love is complete within itself. It cannot be threatened from within, because the lovers are religiously certain of the ecstasy of their love. How then does Shakespeare develop a structure around such a dramatically unpromising center? Largely through the method of antithesis, which slowly in the structural development of the tragedy serves to isolate the lovers, finally driving them to the point of complete isolation, death.

This antithetical structure can be found on several levels: (1) the love-hate action; (2) the youth-age action; (3) the ideal-real love action, and (4) the fate-free will action. The love of Romeo and Juliet, as the Prologue solemnly tells us, is to be understood as a public event. Therefore, it must struggle with the hate of the lovers' families. The feud functions as the source of hatred against which the love must survive. Tybalt is the quintessence of this hatred, and he is explained in medical terms as a victim of his "humor," of choler. But as a character, he is one-dimensional; and that dimension is hatred. He is in the play for no other reason than to dramatize the feud of the Montagues and Capulets. This feud extends to the servants as well as to the lesser members of the two houses. Most tragically, even the citizens of Verona must struggle with this insane war so helplessly out of hand, and finally even the Prince feels the effect of the hatred in the loss of his two kinsmen, Mercutio and Paris. Against this hate, then, the lovers are realized as creatures of irony that, out of such families, they should emerge and redeem in their private love the whole public society of Verona.

The age of Romeo and Juliet is important because it emphasizes the speed which acts as one instrument of Fate in the tragedy. To accentuate its importance, Shakespeare made Juliet younger than the girl in Brooke's poem, his source. Another manner of accenting this feature of age was to place the young lovers in a world ruled by old people. The Capulets and the Montagues cannot penetrate the meaning of such ideal love, or love which is not economically marketable. Only Friar Laurence can understand, but as Romeo points out in Act III, Scene 3, the priest cannot understand the intensity of the young man's passion and ideal love. Again the lovers are isolated. In the important counterpoint of the sexual realism dramatized by the Nurse, Mercutio, and the servants in the first scene, Shakespeare tests the idealism of the love of Romeo and Juliet. These scenes of bawdry and cynicism not only provide comic relief but actually make the audience, saturated in the realism of physical love, believe in the love expressed by the lyricism of the private encounters of the lovers. Shakespeare's antithetical structure, therefore, allows for the central dramatic action of their love, as expressed in heightened poetry, to be believed as real. Thus, the lovers are believed to be truly different, truly isolated from the other characters of the play. Finally, the lovers are isolated by their own fateful circumstances. Seeing each other as "stars," that is, as creatures who can shape their own wills and who can make their own fate, Romeo and Juliet as "stars" have, as their antithesis, the "stars" of Fate. The Prologue had called them "star-crossed lovers" and Romeo, on learning of Juliet's death, declares that he will defy the "stars." The lovers then are structured against the forces of accident and chance which Fate controls for the purposes of Providence. Their ultimate victory in death over the "stars" of Fate is to apotheosize them or make them true "stars" or saints, as the Prince calls them at the end of the play. The result of all four levels of antithesis is to give the structure of the tragedy, in which the main action of the love of Romeo and Juliet is revealed, a powerful effect of dramatic irony.

Question 2.

What are the crucial scenes of the play? Where is the turning point of the dramatic action?

Answer

The crucial scenes of the play are three. The whole of the First Act builds to the encounter of the lovers at the Capulet Feast. With this last scene of the First Act should be included the so-called "balcony scene" (Act II, Scene 2) which immediately follows the first meeting of Romeo and Juliet. These two scenes, included as one, form the first of the crucial scenes. The second scene crucial to the development of the action is Act III, Scene 1, in which Mercutio is killed by Tybalt and then Tybalt is killed by Romeo. The third crucial scene is the last of the tragedy, the suicides of the two lovers. There are many other scenes which are important in furthering the dramatic action (for example, the wedding in Friar Laurence's cell) and also in completing the sequence of several events (for example, the nuptial night and the lyric speeches of the lovers at dawn), but each of these three scenes is the logical culmination of dramatic action. Each is carefully prepared for in Shakespeare's dramatic construction. The last scene is, one might say, the whole purpose of the play: the sacrificial death that unites the feuding families and brings peace to the social fabric of Verona. The crucial turning-point of the play occurs in Act III, Scene 1. With Mercutio's death, the play can no longer sustain comic elements of any length. The death of such a sympathetic character would demand a compensation of mood. Romeo therefore kills Tybalt, and his cry "O, I am Fortune's fool!" is his own recognition that "this day's black fate on more days doth depend;/ This but begins the woe others must end." The only solution to the drama after this scene will be tragic. Romeo's love (the Force A which has been gaining) is now overcome by the power of the feud and Fate itself (Force B, which had been losing in the gradual love of Romeo and Juliet, but has now acquired new directions in the plot).

Question 3.

How do Friar Laurence and Prince Escalus function in the structure of the tragedy?

Answer

Prince Escalus appears only three times in the play, each time to quell the disturbance to the social order of Verona caused by the Capulets and Montagues. His speeches, their stately blank verse often rhymed, dramatize his role as dispenser of justice in Verona. He represents an outside, impersonal force which directs the society in which the lovers commit themselves eternally to their passion. He represents the ultimate reason behind the political order. But ironically, he is powerless in his great authority. He is not severe enough in his initial punishments, and the feud breaks out again. The final result is that he too is drawn into the battle through the loss of his two kinsmen, Mercutio and Paris, Finally, it is not political justice but sacrificial love that can change the order of hate in Verona.

Friar Laurence clearly represents spiritual authority, the voice of inherited wisdom, in the tragedy. But one would do well to see the difference between the wisdom of Friar Laurence's words and the powerlessness of his own actions and perceptions in the tragedy. His admonitions to Romeo about his passion are clearly Shakespeare's intellectual statements about Romeo's tragic flaw. His first homily about the herbs he is gathering in the July dawn is also clearly an answer to the problem of Romeo's misuse of his reason, of his "virtue." He is also obviously Romeo's true father, and Romeo, as he says when leaving the Friar for the last time, genuinely loves his confessor. But the Friar does not understand the passionate intensity of Romeo's love. His intellectualizing reveals his blindness to its mystery. Further, his abandonment of Juliet in the tomb, knowing that she, like Romeo, had come to suicide before, reveals not so much weakness of moral fibre as simple confusion. If, therefore, he does seem absurd at times, one must also remember that in the play as Shakespeare wrote it, he is the clear voice of spiritual authority who intends through the union of the lovers to redeem Verona. Like the Prince, he thus functions as an ultimate authority in the play.

Characters

Character Sketches

Although there is a more complex discussion of the characters in the answers to the questions, these brief descriptions will help the student pinpoint each major character.

Romeo

Romeo is a boy probably almost twenty, a member of the ruling aristocracy of Verona. He is a Montague, and like all Italian noblemen, he has been educated to defend the honor of his family and class. The first view of Romeo is the young man in love with love; his knowledge of the technique of courtly love and of the Neo-Platonic base of such love shows his education. He is easily given to the passion of melancholy, and in the eyes of some critics, his final suicide is the climax of such despair and melancholy. Juliet transforms him into a creature of action, and his response to her love is a measure of his depth of spirit. This response finds its clearest expression in language. It is significant that, throughout the play, Romeo and extravagant language, especially conceits, are related. Equally significant, the language deepens as Romeo's dramatic situation deepens, and what seems artificial in the first view of Romeo is overwhelmingly real in the final scene in the Capulet vault.

Juliet

Juliet is a girl of fourteen, a fact clearly emphasized by Shakespeare, the daughter and only heiress of the Capulet family, one of the ruling powers of Verona. She is devoted to her family by instinct and training as a girl of the Italian aristocracy of the late Middle Ages might be. Her conflict between devotion to family and love for Romeo is the first major obstacle to her marriage to Romeo, as her response to the news of Tybalt's death reveals. But Juliet is a creature of strong and intelligent will. She is especially sensitive to practical possibilities and the threat of violence. In fact, the very intensity of her love for Romeo is always revealed in her willingness to undertake some violent action, as, for example, her drinking of the drug and finally her suicide.

Mercutio

Mercutio is the most charming character in the play. His wit and sexual wordplay are generated by his genuine friendship for Romeo and his concern for the effects of Romeo's love melancholy. He is a little higher in the social scale, actually, than Romeo or Juliet since he is a close kinsman of the ruling Prince, Escalus. His death is as ironic as his language: he is killed as a result of the family feud in which he is a neutral. His Queen Mab speech is one of the great passages of the tragedy. The speech reveals that burst of imagination and of generosity that always marks one of Shakespeare's own favorite characters. As a bachelor friend, Mercutio tries to laugh Romeo out of his love melancholy. The irony of his death is that he dies rebuking Romeo, and without knowing about Romeo's new found love for Juliet. His death is the turning-point of the play.

Friar Laurence

Friar Laurence is a Franciscan priest who lives in Verona and represents, in the tragedy, the voice of spiritual authority. He advises the young lovers in their various and "star-crossed" plots, and both Romeo and Juliet respect and love him as their true father. It is fitting, therefore, that he should marry them and present to both, esecially Romeo, the philosophic world picture which forms the intellectual base of the tragedy. The priest, however, tends to be rather abstract in his advice; and it is clear that he cannot understand the intensity of the love of Romeo and Juliet. If at times he seems absurd and even shows cowardice in leaving Juliet before the guards arrive in the final scene, he is nevertheless the official voice of morality in the play and the student must study his comments carefully in order to calculate the true effect of the tragedy.

The Nurse

The Nurse forms, like Mercutio, an important counterpoint of realism in the play. She is the old servant in the Capulet household who has reared Juliet, even suckling her as a baby. Her morality is worldly, and she has no scruples, for example, about Juliet's having two husbands at once. Her sexual bawdy complements, like Mercutio's, the idealism of the lovers. She is an important member of the Capulet household, as evidenced in the wedding preparation scenes. Ultimately derived from Roman comedy and Commedia dell'Arte, she functions as a go-between for the lovers and, as in the scene with Peter, reveals her own talent for farce.

Lord Capulet

Lord Capulet is the father of Juliet and the head of one of the two ruling families of Verona. He is a bustling figure, as we see in the tireless activity of the man. This sense of hurly-burly is dramatized in language that is often extravagant and conceited but suited to the vitality of the character. He rebukes Tybalt at the Capulet feast because of his genuine desire for peace and because of the honor of his home. His harsh rebuke of Juliet can be understood only by his great love of his only child. A man like Capulet would be mystified by the sharp defiance of a daughter he had always adored. In general, Capulet functions in the play as an Elizabethan father and as the rich London merchants who would have attended a performance of the tragedy at the Globe.

Methods Of Analyzing Character

1. The Basic Facts

The previous descriptions of characters will help to establish the basic facts without which the little world of Verona is impenetrable. For example, it is as important to know that Prince Escalus is the leading political power in an Italian city state as it is to be aware that Othello is a Moor and Macbeth a medieval ruler of Scotland in order to penetrate *Othello* and *Macbeth*. Equally, it is valuable to know that Friar Laurence is a member of the Franciscan order of monks within the community of the Roman Catholic Church because the traditional Scholastic teaching of the Friar can be seen in a better perspective. Such descriptions of characters are ways to start the deeper analysis. First, however, one must have the basic facts.

2. Dynamic or Static

There are many ways to analyze characterization in a work of literature. Needless to say, a novelist has different problems in his presentation of character than has the dramatist. The choice of point of view, the all-important problem for a novelist, is of no real importance to Shakespeare. Therefore characterization will tend to be posited on different premises of construction. But in all works of literature, from *The Sound and the Fury* to the *Oresteia* of Aeschylus, there is one general rule: important characters must *develop* in the drama of the narrative. Not all characters do. Some of our favorite characters, in fact, do not. Mrs. Malaprop in Sheridan's *The Rivals* or Mr. Micawber in *David Copperfield* tend to remain, generally speaking, on the same level of development. Similarly such ideal villains, as, for example, Tybalt in *Romeo and Juliet*, remain the very same. But the great characters of literature have shown their greatest moments in their development under the force of the plot. Their heroic natures are revealed in their reactions to the consequences of their own actions or that of others or, as in *Romeo and Juliet*, of Fate, or more likely, of all combined. Therefore, it can be said that there are characters in works which show development and they can consequently be called dynamic. These characters are molded by the world of the drama through which they are passing. Revealing this interchange of forces around (and within) a central character (or characters) is, of course, one of the absolutely primary tasks of any writer. But, as mentioned before, the evidence of centuries of literature reveals that there are also important characters who are more acted upon than acting. Drama especially, with its peculiar demands of time and space, tends to use these static characters. Not merely Tybalt, but Benvolio, Paris, Mercutio, and even the Nurse show a generally static level of movement as far as their essential characterization is concerned. There are, of course, moments of perception, like the Nurse's shock at Juliet's death. But one cannot see any real change in her simple reaction to the event. Static characters, as Shakespeare knew well, serve the purpose, especially important in this play, of accenting the development of the major characters or, in *Romeo and Juliet*, emphasizing the isolation of the lovers. Often these static characters are called thematic characters because, in a quasi-allegorical manner, they tend to carry one intellectual theme or another. Tybalt is a clear example of such a character. Tybalt carries aloft, for the first three acts, the crucial theme of the feud. He is the embodiment of the hatred of the two families, and his "humor" of choler is merely symptomatic of the disease eating at the vitals of Verona. He is an abstraction, and it is impossible to look for psychological roots in his hatred. His author is theatrically more concerned with the dramatic function of such a character and not with the life of the character *per se*. It is not important to know if Tybalt was married or liked pizza. He is a thematic character, serving a dramatic function throughout, and is thus a static character, one dimensional throughout.

3. Motivation

The danger here is that the student will apply to some periods of literature laws of motivation of character that really belong in other periods. More specifically, a frequent error that students (and critics) make is to take principles of psychological theory which are applicable to many serious modern novels and apply such principles to the characters in Shakespearean drama. Important critics like E.E. Stoll and Miss Lily Campbell have shown that such cannot be the case unless the psychological theory is carefully placed in the context of the work itself with its various antecedents. The problem of motivation — that is, the answer to the "why" of the character's behavior — involves, in Shakespearean tragedy, the matter of dramatic presentation in the Elizabethan and Jacobean theater before an audience saturated with its own prejudices. But having made this initial reservation in his mind, the student may well turn to the marvelously human actions of Shakespeare's characters and see their perennial psychological truth, which may or may not agree with modern theory. He can then discern the motives of individual characters, as the dramatic action progresses. The student then, at this stage, may probably hit on a proven truth in good drama (or good fiction, for that matter). Character is plot, and plot is character. In fact, it is often the individual character's individual plot that determines, with all the character's plots, the main plot itself. The motivation of a character is then his own plot, his own active plan to transform the dramatic action. Romeo's plot is to marry Juliet at whatever cost and live (or die) with her at any cost. Friar Laurence's plot is at first to bring peace to the city of Verona through the wedding of the lovers; then he seeks to let Juliet escape to Mantua and have the lovers re-united, and finally, after Romeo's death, he will help Juliet escape to live out her days in a convent. Mercutio's plot is simply to help his friend. But in every case, the individual plots — the motivations of the characters — decide the course of dramatic action called the plot. As Henry James says in "The Art of Fiction," so here in Shakespearean tragedy: the barriers commonly held between plot and character (and other elements of the work of literature) are as artificial and unreal as many national frontiers. Therefore, motivation in a character, whether dynamic or static, can best be understood in the framework of the plot.

4. Relationships

Finally, character in action, or character as plot, demands that the student see the relationships that exist among various characters. The relationships not only serve to compare and contrast characters, especially the more important figures, but also to set off thematic groups. In *Romeo and Juliet*, the ironic development of the dramatic action depends on just such antithetical groupings of characters. Also, the level of relationship helps the student to understand the social standing of characters in the play. The effect can often be comic as, in the Second Act of *Romeo and Juliet*, when the Nurse is seen commanding Peter, actually her equal. In *Romeo and Juliet*, however, the effect is more often serious because the social tragedy of Verona demands a clear analysis of the social standing of the characters. Finally, the relationships often help us to understand how the major character functions, for example, how Romeo is alive and attractive in his friendship with his bachelor friends. At the same time, as in *Romeo and Juliet*, such relationships might help to show the opposite, as, for example, the isolation of the lovers.

Questions and Answers on the Characters of *Romeo and Juliet*

Question 4.

Discuss the development and motivation of Romeo and Juliet as characters in the tragedy

Answer

It should be said, first of all, that the love of Romeo and Juliet for each other never changes. From the first moment of the sonnet-encounter and from the formal exchange in the Capulet garden, there is no "progression." It is an absolute in the dramatic action, and its ideal nature, or its stasis, provides the isolated nucleus of their existence. In this sense, then, one might say that there is no development in their love. In the little time of the tragedy, Romeo and Juliet never drop the initial intensity found in the first scenes. Juliet vows, then, that she will have her wedding bed as a grave if Romeo is married. Romeo immediately scales the Capulet wall, an invitation to certain death, as Juliet warns him in the balcony scene. Their suicides at the end of the tragedy, therefore, are simply logical developments from this same intensity of love.

In another sense, however, the lovers do develop, and they show this development through their response to the heavy forces of Society and Fate that weigh upon this essentially static center of their love. Romeo has his deepest attack of love melancholy in Friar Laurence's cell after he learns of his exile, and, equally, he is at his manliest when he has fulfilled his love in the nuptial night and must flee. After that point, his strange quietness and brevity of phrase (for example, his almost curt response to the news of Juliet's "death") bespeak and prove that the center of his existence, his love, has intensified and tightened. He can only act in response to that love. Certainly this kind of Romeo, literally deadly serious, is a different creature from the Romeo of the first scene, thrusting conceits and oxymora into the air. The two contrasting kinds of melancholy, one almost a joke and the other an encounter with death in the Capulet tomb, reveals the tightening of character in Romeo. This intensification is the result of Romeo's response to outward circumstance, i.e. the plot in conflict with his, and it is a marked development. Finally this development reveals itself most obviously, as does so much of the play, in the language. The artificial and extravagant phrases of the first scenes still linger in the speeches to Death in the last scene, but the artificiality is purged by the truth of the dramatic situation. The language, therefore, becomes compelling and moving because Romeo is now faced with the most terrible encounter of any man, his own death.

Juliet shows this same development in her almost maternal protection of their love. Her love, she said at the Capulet feast, had a "prodigious birth." She therefore faces any trial to protect its radiant light in the world of darkness. Her most terrible scene is the moment when she is deserted by Father, Mother, and finally her Nurse. At that moment her isolation is brought home to her, and the girl viewed at the first of the tragedy, surrounded by Lady Capulet and her Nurse, has vanished forever. Finally, the complete loneliness required for the taking of the drug is the dramatization of her development. One would have expected of the tough-minded girl of the sonnet-encounter and the witty balcony scene such a possibility of violent action. But her suffering is proof of the development of her character as it changes and transforms itself to protect the center of her existence, the stasis of the lovers' love. The center is static, but her character protecting that center is dynamic and isolates itself ever more to protect that center, even in the isolated death of self-destruction.

Question 5.

What is the dramatic purpose of the character of Benvolio?

Answer

Benvolio is a good example of a static character. He functions to implement the bachelor background of Romeo, to serve as a backdrop to the view of the young lover as a social creature with friends and family. His remarks in the various scenes with Romeo and Mercutio often serve as foils for Mercutio's and Romeo's jokes or declamations. He is gentler with Romeo than Mercutio because he tends to understand Romeo's desire to seek the night (there is an implication in his first speech that he too has known love melancholy) and the devices of the lovesick. But he is just as determined to rid Romeo, his dear friend and cousin, of this dangerous illness. It is his plan, ironically, that rids Romeo of Rosaline and leads him into the arms of Juliet. When Shakespeare no longer needs a foil for Romeo, he drops Benvolio. The last we see of this faithful friend is in Act III when he advises Romeo to flee.

Question 6.

Discuss Shakespeare's use of decorum in the characterization of the play.

Answer

The opening episode of the play has servants fighting servants. This comic beginning is signaled by the use of prose, always the medium for comedy and for the speech of characters from the lower levels of society. Decorum, or appropriateness, of tone is the law governing such a level of speech and action. The difference is also rendered in the next action of the opening scene, the arrival of Benvolio and Tybalt, members of the aristocracy who speak in the language suited to such figures, blank verse. Finally, Prince Escalus, the highest peak of Verona society, enters, and his speech, blank verse larded with metaphors and other figures of speech and rhyme, reflects the difference in social level not only from the servants but also from the middle aristocracy represented by the Capulets and Montagues. Similarly, Friar Laurence's speeches reveal his level as spiritual authority. He speaks sententiously, often in rhymed blank verse (which tends in this play to represent impersonal sentiment).

Question 7.

How is Paris motivated in the dramatic action? Why is he killed at the end?

Answer

Paris supplies something of the function of what Henry James called a *ficelle*. That is, Paris helps to develop the central action and to provide a kind of counterpart to a major character, in this case Romeo. It should be remembered, first of all, that he is neither Capulet nor Montague. He is, in fact, Mercutio's kinsman, a member of the Prince's family. He genuinely loves Juliet, a fact attested to by his constant pursuit of her, by his loving dialogue with her at Friar Laurence's cell, but most clearly by his devotion at her tomb. His touching elegy and his desire to cleanse her tomb and keep watch over it are proofs of the depth of his love for Juliet. Therefore, Romeo is right when he calls him brother in this last scene. But why should he be killed? Critics have found it a problem in the play for the death is Shakespeare's own invention; it occurs in none of the other versions. Briefly, it seems that Romeo's violence, later to be used against himself, definitely shows its possibilities when it so quickly kills Paris. The violence of that death seems to accentuate Romeo's state of despair at the tomb, the complete result of his love melancholy.

Question 8.

Discuss the Nurse as a stock character.

Answer

A stock character is usually a character derived from convention and may often be a static character. In this case, the Nurse derives from the old bawd or procuress of the Roman comedy of Plautus and Terence and also from the character of the *ruffiana* or bawd in the Commedia dell'Arte. She also functions like the servants in Roman comedy who act as go-betweens for the major characters. Those scenes in which she delays to tell Juliet key information are scenes ultimately derived from Roman comedy. But the important point is that Shakespeare took such a stock character from ancient traditions and gave it the life that only old Angelica — a name ringing with irony — has in all of English literature. Her bawdry serves a vital schematic purpose in the drama; her realism of language heightens the lyric language of the lovers by providing ironic contrast; and her farcical actions, if derived from Roman comedy and the Commedia dell'Arte, are completely English slapstick and perform an important function in the dramatic construction of the tragedy.

Meaning
Methods Of Analyzing Meaning
Why meaning at all?

The significance of a literary work depends ultimately on its "idea," as discussed in the previous section on structure. The structural concept of the work, its form in the broadest sense, its "idea," will be its meaning in a very real sense. But there are certain shapings of material that allow the student to see that an author intends this or that theme to be predominant and to give his plot a special meaning. It is possible, consequently, for the student to generalize as his generalization springs out of the concrete text before him. In fact, it is really bad for any student to be so caught up in details that he cannot — or worse, is afraid to — generalize on the ultimate meaning of literary works. Literature is not written in isolation. The writer and his characters are entities formed from laws of economics, of politics, of religion, and of biology. To fail to see that the author might possess a bias is the worst kind of analysis. Good writers are seldom antiseptic. They generally have more emotions and a greater range of feeling in general than the average reader. They often, therefore, have predispositions toward political theories or religious beliefs that can both limit and enrich their views. No writer would be happy with the unemotional mathematical equations of the computer. He must, in a real sense, believe. But how do these beliefs relate to his work? The danger, obviously, is that the abstract belief overwhelm the concrete material. Often this happens, even in significant works. But more often, as in *Romeo and Juliet*, the philosophical world-picture is integrated into the dramatic action so that, for example, the Friar's homilies — which represent, by and large, the philosophical basis of *Romeo and Juliet* — seem natural and inevitable and help to define, even by their omission, the intensity of the love of Romeo and Juliet. In the long run, then, it is advisable for students to look for meanings, for abstract ideas inherited from systems relevant in the period of the work, but *only* as those ideas are part of the greater "idea," the form of the work.

Where to find meaning

Meaning in a literary work is usually abstracted at first from the themes that run through the work. Where can a student find these themes? The answer is in three areas: (1) in the body of the whole work; (2) in the plot and its complication; and (3) in inherited conventions of expression and idea. First, the meaning is usually perceptible in the beginning and end of a work. These are crucial areas, as any good writer knows. *Romeo and Juliet* is a fine example of how the student is directed toward its ultimate meaning at the very beginning of the tragedy. The Prologue tells us immediately that the meaning of the play is the sacrificial love of the two young people that heals the society of Verona. Here the three great themes of the play are set, and the fullest directions are given for the ultimate solution to the problems set by these three themes. The final scene of the play merely repeats, in the Prince's speeches, what has been announced by the Prologue.

Secondly, meaning also is revealed in the machinations of the plot. In fact, as mentioned before, it is impossible to tell where plot or character ends and meaning begins. All are one in the form of the work. But the complications of the action do show the author's guiding hand (and often even he does not consciously know the significance of what he is doing). Certain scenes and certain characters in these scenes clearly remind us of the deeper significance of the work and take us into the realm of ideas. The dramatic action is so constructed that it is inevitable that the student must see the underlying idea. But there is one serious problem here: logic. It often happens that the student finds that his understanding of the theme simply does not logically fit the implications of the plot. What is he to do? There are two courses that he can follow: (1) either check his theory of the work's meaning more closely with a re-reading of the text or (2) after some exhaustive study, decide that the author himself has not followed the logical implications of his own ideas. Humility demands, especially with a major work, that the student do his work rather thoroughly before coming to the second conclusion. In all cases, the student should refer to the plot and the work itself. The evidence is always in the plot.

Finally, a well-trained student may pick out conventions either of expression or of idea that will be clues to the ultimate meaning of the work. Analyzing a work from the medieval period will demand some sense of the intellectual world-picture of that day, if the meaning is to be even partially grasped. Themes themselves are often conventional and established and can be found if the student has been trained well enough to know the history of such ideas. It is rare, for example, in Shakespeare's day, that a popular work like a theater piece will have an unusual meaning or revolutionary significance. Certainly, Shakespeare's originality, if it does exist, is carefully placed in a context of ideas, all largely inherited from the usual Renaissance sources for its world-picture, the classical world of Greece and Rome and the Judaic-Christian religious tradition. The concept of originality, as the Romantics generally understand that term, does not exist in Shakespeare's world. Therefore, meaning can usually be discovered by the student in three ways: through clues in the body of the whole work; in the direct complications of the plot, and in the conventional ideas and expressions found in the work itself.

Questions And Answers On the Meaning of *Romeo and Juliet*

Question 9

What are the three themes that give the tragedy of Romeo and Juliet its deepest meaning?

Answer

Shakespeare presents the three themes, or levels of meaning of the tragedy, in the opening sonnet-speech of the Prologue: Fate, Society, and the private love of Romeo and Juliet. Everything in the play finds its meaning in the logical (one might almost say mathematical) relationship of these three themes. The force of Fate is signaled throughout the play by an intricate series of premonitions, uttered by the major characters Romeo and Juliet, and also by Friar Laurence. None of the other characters make these premonitions, but their force is given ironically in the various actions that appear as coincidences or accidents. For example, seeing the servant give Romeo the guest-list of the Capulet feast, the audience, having heard from the Prologue that the lovers will die, will feel the force of premonition in the dramatic irony of the event. But the most insistent means by which the audience feels the power of Fate, over and beyond the will of the characters, is in Shakespeare's use of speed in the dramatic action. Literally the form of the play is a matter of time, as the Prologue tells us, "two hours' traffic." Shakespeare continues this sense of whirling action in the fight of the servants, in Paris' urgent suit, the instant love of the two lovers, in the reference to their youth, in the immediate exchange of vows in the Capulet orchard and the plans for marriage, in the swift exchange between Tybalt and Mercutio and the death of both, in Romeo's flight, in the hurried plans for the marriage with Paris (the Capulet household literally bursting with speed for fear that time will overtake them), the suddenness with which Romeo learns of Juliet's "death," and finally the speed of the events in the Capulet tomb. Always and everywhere the characters seem to be in a hurry or acting for others who are in haste. This speed then forms dramatic evidence of the force of Fate.

But the meaning of the play is not merely fatalistic. The Prologue tells us that Fate operates in the play as an instrument of Providence. What does this mean? It is obvious that the conventional background of ideas here is that of the Judaic-Christian world that believes not a sparrow falls without the direct intervention of God. Of course, man has free will, as one of Friar Laurence's little sermons — always the best source, with the Prince's speeches, for the conventional sources of meaning — tells us. This "rude will" can dominate "grace," however; that is, the free passion can overcome reason or the voice of God in man, if passion is not controlled. The result is death, as Friar Laurence says in his speech of the Second Act. In the Shakespearean universe the student must forget the opposition to be found, for example in the novels of Thomas Hardy: the opposition of fate and providence. This is nineteenth-century secularism, and whatever its value, this view of the universe is not Shakespeare's. Fate *is* Providence in *Romeo and Juliet*. As the Prologue tells us, Providence uses the instruments of Fate to accomplish its own good ends, that is, the renewal of the society of Verona. There is, therefore, a Providence who can use accident and coincidence with all their terrible ironies for an end of love (not the irony of Hardy that depicts either complete despair or nobility before nothingness, as Tess at Stonehenge). The Elizabethans had as an official belief that the universe was completely rational because God had created every single bit of it with love. This is not to say that they thought it could be understood by man; nor that the official belief was so firmly held in an age when all beliefs were crumbling. But it is the obvious first meaning of *Romeo and Juliet* that Providence uses the force of Fate for its own benign ends.

Society is the recipient of the good ends of Providence. Verona has been rent by the bloody feud of the Montagues and Capulets, "where civil blood makes civil hands unclean." It is good to recall here that Shakespeare's tragedies are always public. Convention demanded that any serious action be displayed in the public realm. A private theme could never have enough relevance to be tragic. Tragedy automatically implied the social. Such a concept is implied in Aristotle, and the tragedy of individual love simply would not be relevant enough for an Elizabethan. Therefore, Shakespeare sets up the second great theme in the public realm. The forces of family and of political justice are juxtaposed to the love of two teenagers, and such great forces, with all their economic, political and social demands, crush the lovers in a few days. Shakespeare never ceases to dramatize this social theme. The first scene shows even the servants involved in feud; the discussion of Capulet and Paris shows how Juliet is really an economic commodity and, furthermore, the great weight of family position in Verona; the social dimension is revealed fully in the Capulet feast and in the later preparations for the second wedding; the great hold of the family name is rendered in Juliet's immediate reaction at the news of Tybalt's death; when Capulet later threatens Juliet, the audience might gasp in terror because the Elizabethans knew the fate of an aristocratic girl thrown into the streets. These are a few of the many uses of the public dimension of the tragedy. Prince Escalus is the official voice of the suffering society of Verona; and Friar Laurence, as its spiritual authority, seeks the wedding of Romeo and Juliet as a means of healing the wounds. But Providence acting through Fate is stronger than either of the two social voices. It has its own plan of redemption.

The third theme of the tragedy is the love of Romeo and Juliet themselves. This force is an absolute, as already suggested, and it operates as seemingly defeated by the immense pressures of Fate and Society. But, as Donald Stauffer has pointed out, love acts as schoolmaster to society. Or, ironically, the belief of Romeo and Juliet in their ideal love is so absolute that it does, in a real sense, transcend its own private nature and turn upon its oppressors, Society and Fate, and give direction and meaning to both. Society is renewed by the absolute belief in love that Romeo and Juliet have. No great political, economic, or socio-religious forces have been able to heal the feud and the hatred. The healing comes only from the love of two teenagers who have not yielded in their absolute devotion to the ideal of love. Even Fate, with its instruments of accident and chance, is outwitted. Love, as revealed in the balcony scene and in the dawn farewells, is stronger than the force of coincidence. Providence itself is renewed by the act of love which it has precipitated. This third theme, then, of the ideal love of Romeo and

Juliet is the real center of the tragedy, affected by the two forces of Fate and Society and itself affecting these two great forces.

Question 10.

How does Shakespeare dramatize the meaning of this third theme?

Answer

The intensity of the love of Romeo and Juliet is, as critics have pointed out, the real ethical energy of the tragedy. Friar Laurence, the Prologue, and Prince Escalus give official moralizings. But the absolute nature of this love dominates the lyric heights of the finest scenes of the play. It is clear that from the standpoint of experience, if not of moral philosophy, the private lyric intensity of the lovers is the moral center of the drama. How can Shakespeare render this fact and show that it is public and redemptive? He dramatizes this moral center through a skillful manipulation of conventional ideas. From the beginning, Romeo and Juliet have addressed each other as saints (or pilgrims). Romeo is literally wearing a pilgrim's costume at the Capulet feast when he meets Juliet. This motif of the lovers as saints, introduced so lightly in the high comedy of the first scenes, works slowly through the tragedy until the final scene when the sacrificial death of the lovers is revealed. Whatever the ultimate outcome of their suicide (damnation in the eyes of the Roman Catholic Church), their love has been redemptive. For these two lovers, therefore, both fathers will erect statues of pure gold and the entire citizenry of Verona will commemorate them. In short, Romeo and Juliet have literally become saints in the little world of the play. Shakespeare, with consummate craftsmanship, has made the center of the play, the love, not only truly absolute in itself (by assuming the nature of sanctity — a condition an Elizabethan audience could believe in) but public and relevant to society. The imagery of sainthood has managed to suggest both the eternal, temporal, social, and private nature of their love. Like true saints, they have also overcome death. The conventional meanings of the invocations to death that recur in the play, especially in the final scene in the Capulet tomb, are also put in the framework of the saint imagery. Death itself is subject to love. Their love, the scene implies, will overcome even death through its redemptive powers. Ironically, in their death-marriage they will best serve life by redeeming it through sacrificial love, like true saints.

Question 11.

Discuss the meaning of Romeo's melancholy. Is this Romeo's tragic flaw? Is Shakespeare logical in the extended meaning of this flaw?

Answer

From the first scene of the play, the audience is made acutely aware

102

of Romeo's love melancholy. Later Romeo is told to purge this dangerous passion through finding a new love. He does, and the result is intensification of love, rather than release from the passion. Mercutio's main function, it would seem, is his desire to tease Romeo out of this dangerous state. Probably the clearest scene where love melancholy expresses itself occurs in Friar Laurence's cell when Romeo learns of his exile. His despair, his outcries, and his prostration on the floor elicit the sharpest rebuke by Friar Laurence and the sharpest philosophical attack on such a dangerous passion. Finally, the melancholy is seen in Romeo's invocation of death in the tomb scene and in the violence revealed in his murdering Paris. What does all this mean? Obviously, Shakespeare intends for the audience to see Romeo as a slave of passion, lost in its demands, finally killing himself for love. It does operate, therefore, in the tragedy like the *hamartia* or tragic flaw that Aristotle defined as the defect within the hero that brings his downfall. Love melancholy, which the Elizabethans understood in a medical sense as well as moral and ethical, was a dangerous passion. The conventional background of the idea that passion could be dangerous lay in the tenet that classical Rome had evolved in its greatest hero, Aeneas: reason over passion. A human being who has submitted the noble powers of reason to "rude will," as Friar Laurence called it, or passion, could only find death. Love melancholy does operate in the tragedy, then, as Romeo's tragic flaw.

Yet, viewed in the larger perspective of the three themes of the play, it will be immediately clear that Shakespeare has not been entirely consistent in the development of the meaning of the flaw. If Romeo does kill himself in a fit of passion, as implied, how then does one explain the newly transformed Romeo of the last scenes? Further, how can the intensity of the love scenes be merely explained as evil consequences of dangerous passion? These scenes, as stated above, for the moral nucleus of the play. Finally, how can Romeo be seen as a "saint" for his sacrificial act, an act caused by his absolute belief in the power of love, and then have that very love condemned as a tragic flaw? Shakespeare, as Stauffer and other critics have pointed out, is not logical here. He is not clear about Romeo's free will or choice. He confuses our angle of belief in the lovers by giving us two focuses instead of one: the lovers as "saints," clearly the truer meaning (if we are to judge the text as evidence), and the lovers as victims of their own love-melancholy (resulting in their suicides and possible external damnation), the official philosophy of the tragedy. It is precisely this blurring that keeps *Romeo and Juliet* from being one of Shakespeare's very great tragedies.

Style

Methods Of Analyzing Style

Style is that intangible quality of a literary work that we cannot always define, but can immediately recognize, like the taste of good beer or the smell of fresh herbs. It is brought to our attention by certain devices. These devices are like the materials of a carpenter which we might call the trim or finish of a product. Of course, as the student has been observing all along, nothing in a good work of literature is merely ornament. The stylistic devices operate as closely and as intimately as plot and character and theme. They are, in fact, the very appearance of those elements. It would be foolish, then, to say that such devices operate independently of the little world of the play. In fact, such stylistic devices as diction or imagery cannot exist at all unless the writer shapes them toward a certain end, unless they form part and parcel of the very idea they are expressing. Now, as any good student of literature knows, the writer's shaping of his material is literally a mystery. Even he does not know all about the very process he is involved in. Therefore, style cannot be understood from above, so to speak, like a mathematical formula. One cannot wait like an automaton for some magic computer to pour forth the rules of style. A knowledge of style, in any literary work, comes, quite simply, from reading the work itself — really reading and re-reading, if there is time, in patience and silence and then meditating, just thinking about the very form of the work. Such patience is finally the only way to appreciate style. In the process of patience, a knowledge of the devices used in gaining style will benefit the student and increase that final appreciation of the style of a literary work. Here are some of the devices by which an author develops the element of style:

Diction

Diction is simply the choice of words in a work of literature. Good diction is, as Swift said, the right words in the right places. Certain subjects demand certain kinds of words. It is proper for example, in the novel *Catcher in the Rye* that the diction be colloquial, natural, and conversational. But in *Romeo and Juliet*, another literary work about adolescents, that solemn tone of the Prologue would have told the Elizabethan audience that the tragic consequences demanded such stylistic solemnity, or heightening of expression. Here again, Shakespeare's diction in the play is dependent on his concept of decorum. The socially low comic servants and the young bachelors speak prose with a rough, realistic vocabulary. The lovers speak in heightened blank verse, with involved conceits and with a generally Latinate vocabulary. Friar Laurence and Prince Escalus use a language that is often rhymed blank verse, expressing impersonal sentiments suited to their position of authority. Their choice of words similarly is lofty but direct in its meaning. It should be remembered that *Romeo and Juliet*, *Richard II*, and *Midsummer Night's Dream* are considered Shakespeare's most lyric dramas. This is to say that the effects of language (diction and imagery) are brought to heights which the dramatic situation does not always fully support, but which in themselves are among Shakespeare's greatest.

Imagery

An image in a literary work is a concrete representation of an object capable of being perceived sensuously by the reader. It can, in this broad meaning, be almost any concrete phenomenon in the work, and images can consequently be fixed with meaning or freed in their general connotation. Most frequently the term imagery builds on this sense of concrete representation, but means more specifically figurative language. Figures of speech in a work of literature serve the important purpose of making us understand a scene or a character or an idea better than we would have if the material had been presented simply and literally. For example, in *Romeo and Juliet*, the figures of speech about explosions help the student to form his own understanding of the dangers and intensity of the love of Romeo and Juliet. The comparisons of certain actions in the play to occurrences of explosion are not, in one sense, necessary. The literal facts could have survived without these comparisons. But could they really? Would their meaning have been truly justified? Would, in fact, the literal event have been worth it to us? Ancient poets and rhetoricians, thousands of years ago, saw this instinctive human effort to relate experience of one thing to experience of another as a mark of civilization. Through the classical schools of Greece and Rome, consequently, grew up an elaborate system of figures of speech which the Renaissance, both in its inheritance from the Middle Ages and in its nature as a revival of ancient classical wisdom, took as its own. It was natural that Shakespeare should use such figures of speech in his plays for he had been taught them every day in his Latin grammar school. As mentioned above, *Romeo and Juliet* is considered one of Shakespeare's most lyric plays. The use of figures of speech, therefore, would be a key instrument by which such lyric heights could be revealed. *Throughout the preceding summaries and comments on the plot will be found identifications of figures of speech and their definitions. The student should refer to these.*

Emphasis

The concept of arrangement is perhaps more a matter of structure than style. But style is formed on just such a balance of emphasis. For example, it is hard for any student to appreciate the subtlety of Hawthorne's *The Scarlet Letter* unless he can see how carefully Hawthorne has arranged the elements of the scene in the forest where Hester Prynne and Dimmesdale meet and how carefully the points of emphasis are developed. The author knows just how much time is to be spent on the trivial and, similarly, on the symbolic. This kind of arrangement, which naturally involves elements of syntax and diction and figures of speech, is what one calls emphasis of style. Shakespeare is a master of this handling of scene. A glance at the scene in which Juliet cries out her epithalamium only to be met by the Nurse's terrible news about Tybalt's death will show how Shakespeare manages the texture or style of the whole scene by arrangement of various emphases. In a novel or short story or narrative poem, such emphasis could be gained by the use of point of view, or deciding who is telling the story, a problem not too relevant in Shakespearean drama. More relevant is the fact that emphasis can also be judged by contrasting the arrangements of a certain scene with that of another so that the style of the whole play or novel can be viewed as a unity. With great writers as Shakespeare, the student can go even further. He can compare the style of one work with that of another, and see how the various levels of emphasis relate or contrast. Finally, from emphasis (and with it the element of arrangement called coherence or holding together), one can guess at certain subjective elements of style, a certain bias revealing itself in arrangement. But such guesses are dangerous and hardly worth the immense labor that one must expend to find a true answer. As always, the best place to look for emphasis of style is in the plot, the work of literature as it is alive in action. Style springs from the living organism of the work of art, not from externals.

Convention

There are certain literary forms that have been handed down and used in literary works of different periods. *Romeo and Juliet*, as a lyric work deliberately emphasizing its "poetic" and linguistic effects, uses several of these. These forms, like the figures of speech, are expressions of style. This is to say that they are inherited forms which are made integral in the plot or dramatic action of the work. Many literary works employ as devices of style such conventional forms. For example, it should always be clear to any student of Shakespeare that his works are primarily written in blank verse, unrhymed iambic pentameter. This conventional basis of style is, however, varied and can range from the most prosaic passages to the most varied and exalted of verse forms, such as the songs in *Midsummer Night's Dream* and *The Tempest*. These conventions are not always linguistic, however. The convention of the Chorus in *Romeo and Juliet* is an inherited stylistic device from the Greeks and Romans. Generally, all these conventions are more specific in their use than, for example, the figures of speech which are more easily adaptable.

Questions And Answers On Style
In *Romeo and Juliet*

Question 12.

Comment upon the extravagant diction that characterizes certain characters of the play, for example, Romeo and Lord Capulet.

Answer

It is true that old Capulet seems at times to use a vocabulary unsuited to his hurly-burly nature. For example, when he sees Juliet weeping in the last scene of the Third Act, he bursts into the most fanciful kinds of comparisons: her body is a ship, a sea, and a wind. The language here seems out of place as later his laments with his wife's and the Nurse's wails seem unsuited as reactions to the drugged sleep of Juliet. Such language is like that of the "rude mechanicals" in their presentation of the tragic love story of Pyramus and Thisbe in *Midsummer Night's Dream*. It is too artificial for the demands of the dramatic situation. We cannot believe in it. Students today must remember that the early Shakespeare wrote for an audience that loved bombast and extravagant rhetoric. The later Shakespeare was to learn how to handle such scenes, but Elizabethan drama was built on exaggeration and Shakespeare had first to learn how to use it, not to discard it. Romeo's first speeches are extravagant, but as commented on already, such extravagant diction becomes increasingly more real as the situation of the dramatic action tightens. In the final scene in the Capulet tomb, Romeo's invocations to death are artificial in themselves but quite moving because of the pathos of the dramatic situation.

Question 13.

Identify the various forms of verse used in *Romeo and Juliet*.

Answer

The tragedy has generally three levels of language: prose, blank verse, and rhymed verse. With important exceptions, the prose is the language of servants and comedy; the blank verse, for the personal and more intimate scenes (the love scenes with their rhymes are obvious exceptions); and the rhymed verse, for the impersonal and generalized scenes. But embedded within the tragedy there are four conventional forms of lyric verse:

1. *Sonnet*   There are three sonnets in the play. The Chorus speaks the first in his Prologue to Act I and he speaks the third sonnet in the Prologue to Act II. The second sonnet forms the linguistic encounter of Romeo and Juliet at the Capulet feast. All three are examples of the English or Shakespearean sonnet with the rhyme scheme of ababcdcdefefgg, that is, three quatrains (four line sections of a poem) and a couplet. The sonnet form was traditionally used at this period for love poetry. It was derived from the Italian poet, Petrarch, whom Mercutio satirizes in the fourth scene of Act II.

2. *Epithalamium*   Juliet's soliloquy in the beginning of the second scene of Act III is an example of a wedding song or *epithalamium*. She is praising her wedding of the afternoon and anticipating the consum-

mation of her love in the nuptial night. This is the traditional subject matter of an *epithalamium*, which, in English, can assume any metric form. Because this soliloquy is one of anticipation and waiting, it might also be called a *serena*, a lyric recited in romances by the lady as she awaited her beloved in the evening.

3. *Aubade*   The dialogue of the two lovers in the dawning of their nuptial night (the last scene of Act III) is an excellent example of a song sung at dawn, often as lamentation by lovers at the end of the night of love. This *alba* or *aube* or *aubade* can have any metric form in English.

4. *Elegy*   Paris' speech in the final scene, as he approaches Juliet's tomb and throws flowers over its entrance, is an example of a poem celebrating the dead, or an *elegy*. The poem could take any form in English, often as an ode, but here it is a simple rhymed lyric set into the blank verse of the scene.

Question 14.

Do the elements of comedy in the tragedy show an appropriate emphasis?

Answer

There are, generally speaking, two kinds of comedy in the play: the low comedy of the servants, ending usually in some sort of slapstick and farce, and the high comedy of repartee and verbal duels. This first type of comedy is found at key points: the first scene, the household scenes of the Capulet feast and the wedding preparations (both scenes involving important dramatic action), the scene in which Juliet's body is discovered (where Peter and the musicians joke), and the action of the cowardly page in the final scene. In every case this kind of low comedy involving servants takes its cue from its origin in Roman comedy and provides the style with broad humor. It serves, in the structure and style, as comic relief to the almost unbearably pathetic scenes which it often frames. Between the two areas of high and low comedy lies the comedy of the Nurse and Mercutio. The Nurse tends to be part of the low comedy, but she is much more rounded as a character than, for example, Peter. She can suffer, and she can give advice. But she too, as already commented upon, serves as antithesis with her bawdy low comedy and her characteristics of an old peasant woman. Mercutio naturally belongs to the level of high comedy because he possesses *par excellence* the gift of gab. But he too is involved in horseplay and the kind of active humor associated with farce, although it is his verbal wit and the sexual jokes that the student best remembers. At the other end of high comedy, there is the verbal dueling of Romeo and Juliet in their various encounters. Progressively their scenes together cease to have the lightness of the verbal duel of Shakespeare's lovers in the romantic comedies. But the sonnet-encounter at Capulet's feast does reveal an important side of both: their readiness to act in a social situation and to respond with intelligence to their own emotions. The audience needs to see these characters as rounded. Therefore, stylistically at least, they must first be presented as figures from a high comedy before their tragedy is unfolded. In both cases, the style of the play is intensified by the emphasis of comedy, both low and high.

Question 15.

Briefly explain three dominant patterns of imagery in *Romeo and Juliet*.

Answer

The most comprehensive of all patterns of imagery is that contrasting light and darkness. From the first view of Romeo in his love melancholy, the student will be aware of this contrast. Romeo seeks, says Benvolio, "artificial night." It is climaxed in the tomb scene where in the darkness of death the lovers become a kind of eternal light to each other and to Verona. The balcony scene and the dawning song are two places in the dramatic action where the pattern is most visually dramatized. But the whole imagery of the stars is part of this pattern; and the student can find innumerable references. The clearest expression of the imagery of light and darkness, as Caroline Spurgeon has indicated, is in the lightning image which Juliet first uses for their love in the balcony scene. This image of sudden brilliant light in darkness is one of the best visual expressions of the whole sense of intensity in the love of Romeo and Juliet.

The lightning image leads to a second important image pattern: the explosion imagery. As it can be readily seen, this explosion imagery is akin to the larger light-darkness pattern. Like the lightning, it merely expresses the violence of that pattern. But Shakespeare is so precise about his use of explosion imagery that it definitely needs to be examined apart. There are only three places in the play where the explosion image is spelled out although it is clearly implied in other places. The first of these occurs in the last scene of Act II where Friar Laurence admonishes the over-anxious Romeo:

> These violent delights have violent ends
> And in their triumph die, like fire and powder,
> Which as they kiss consume:

The second occurs also in Friar Laurence's cell when Romeo has thrown himself on the floor in despair and then risen, when the Nurse has entered, only to try to commit suicide. In the Friar's long speech, he accuses Romeo of abusing, among other things, his wit or intelligence with the result that his reason:

> Like powder in a skilless soldier's flask,
> Is set afire by thine own ignorance,
> And thou dismembered with thine own defense.

The last of these explosion images is Romeo's. It occurs when he is speaking to the apothecary, and its use implies that Romeo knows the violence he is incurring on himself in passionate surrender to his melancholy. Romeo hopes that he may die quickly:

> And that the trunk may be discharged of breath
> As violently as hasty powder fired
> Doth hurry from the fatal cannon's womb.

The third dominant image pattern, as discussed previously, is the death-marriage imagery. Juliet had referred to her grave as her wedding bed in the first moments after their encounter at the Capulet feast; later their attempted suicides and Juliet's drugged sleep dramatized this image pattern; Capulet and Paris specifically refer to Death the bridegroom as does Juliet implicitly in her soliloquy before taking the poison. But the great scene is the final scene where Death is challenged by Romeo and invoked as he breaks open the entrance to the Capulet vault. The very scene of the vault is the dramatic visualization of the death-marriage image. If this were not enough, Romeo details the effects of death (and their failure to claim Juliet) and finally names Death as her paramour. Ironically, he performs the wedding rite with Death as Lover as does Juliet: the rite of suicide. This famous theme, Gothic and Romantic in later literatures, lives in imagery that literally becomes dramatic action in the plot. The suicides are the Death-Marriage imagery completed and visualized.

Selected Criticisms

This play is one of the most pleasing of our Author's performances. The scenes are busy and various, the incidents numerous and important, the catastrophe irresistibly affecting, and the process of the action carried on with such probability, at least with such congruity to popular opinions, as tragedy requires.

Here is one of the few attemps of *Shakespeare* to exhibit the conversation of gentlemen, to represent the airy sprightliness of juvenile elegance. Mr. *Dryden* mentions a tradition, which might easily reach his time, of a declaration made by *Shakespeare*, that *he was obliged to kill Mercutio in the third act, lest he should have been killed by him.* Yet he thinks him *no such formidable person, but that he might have lived through the play, and died in his bed*, without danger to a poet. *Dryden* well knew, had he been in quest of truth, that, in a pointed sentence, more regard is commonly had to the words than the thought, and that it is very seldom to be rigorously understood. *Mercutio's* wit, gaiety and courage, will always procure him friends that wish him a longer life; but his death is not precipitated, he has lived out the time allotted him in the construction of the play; nor do I doubt the ability of *Shakespeare* to have continued his existence, though some of his sallies are perhaps out of the reach of *Dryden*; whose genius was not very fertile of merriment, nor ductile to humour, but acute, argumentative, comprehensive, and sublime.

The Nurse is one of the characters in which the Author delighted: he has, with great subtilty of distinction, drawn her at once loquacious and secret, obsequious and insolent, trusty and dishonest.

His comick scenes are happily wrought, but his pathetick strains are always polluted with some unexpected depravations. His persons, however distressed, *have a conceit left them in their misery, a miserable conceit.*

Samuel Johnson

Romeo and Juliet is the only tragedy which Shakespear has written entirely on a love-story. It is supposed to have been his first play, and it deserves to stand in that proud rank. There is the buoyant spirit of youth in every line, in the rapturous intoxication of hope, and in the bitterness of despair. It has been said of *Romeo and Juliet* by a great critic, that "whatever is most intoxicating in the odour of a southern spring, languishing in the song of the nightingale, or voluptuous in the first opening of the rose, is to be found in this poem." The description is true; and yet it does not answer to our idea of the play. For if it has the sweetness of the rose, it has its freshness too; if it has the languor of the nightingale's song, it has also its giddy transport; if it has the softness of a southern spring, it is as glowing and as bright. There is nothing of a sickly and sentimental cast. Romeo and Juliet are in love, but they are not love-sick...Their courtship is not an insipid interchange of sentiments lip-deep, learnt at second-hand from poems and plays, — made up of beauties of the most shadowy kind, of "fancies wan that hang the pensive head," of evanescent smiles, and sighs that breathe not, of delicacy that shrinks from the touch, and feebleness that scarce supports itself, an elaborate vacuity of thought, and an artificial dearth of sense, spirit, truth, and nature! It is the reverse of all this. It is Shakespear all over, and Shakespear when he was young.

We have heard it objected to *Romeo and Juliet*, that it is founded on an idle passion between a boy and a girl, who have scarcely seen and can have but little sympathy or rational esteem for one another, who have had no experience of the good or ills of life, and whose raptures or despair must be therefore equally groundless and fantastical. Whoever objects to the youth of the parties in this play as "too unripe and crude" to pluck the sweets of love, and wishes to see a first-love carried on into a good old age, and the passions taken at the rebound, when their force is spent, may find all this done in the *Stranger* and in other German plays, where they do things by contraries, and transpose nature to inspire sentiment and create philosophy. Shakespear proceeded in a more strait-forward, and, we think, effectual way. He did not endeavour to extract beauty from wrinkles, or the wild throb of passion from the last expiring sigh of indifference. He did not "gather grapes of thorns nor figs of thistles." It was not his way. But he has given a picture of human life, such as it is in the order of nature. He has founded the passion of the two lovers not on the pleasures they had experienced, but on all the pleasures they had *not* experienced. All that was to come of life was theirs. At that untried source of promised happiness they slaked their thirst, and the first eager draught made them drunk with love and joy. They were in full possession of their senses and their affections . . . Passion, the love and expectation of pleasure, is infinite, extravagant, inexhaustible, till experience comes to check and kill it. Juliet exclaims on her first interview with Romeo —

My bounty is as boundless as the sea,
My love as deep.

And why should it not? What was to hinder the thrilling tide of pleasure, which had just gushed from her heart, from flowing on without stint or measure, but experience which she was yet without? What was to abate the transport of the first sweet sense of pleasure, which her heart and her senses had just tasted, but indifference which she was yet a stranger to? What was there to check the ardour of hope, of faith, of constancy, just rising in her breast, but disappointment which she had not yet felt! As are the desires and hopes of youthful passion, such is the keenness of its disappointments, and their baleful effect. Such is the transition in this play from the highest bliss to the lowest despair, from the nuptial couch to an untimely grave. The only evil that even in apprehension befalls the two lovers is the loss of the greatest possible felicity; yet this loss is fatal to both, for they had rather part with life than bear the thought of surviving all that had made life dear to them. In all this, Shakespear has but followed nature, which existed in his time, as well as now. The modern philosophy, which reduces the whole theory of the mind to habitual impressions, and leaves the natural impulses of passion and imagination out of the account, had not then been discovered; or if it had, would have been little calculated for the uses of poetry...In youth and boyhood, the world we live in is the world of desire, and of fancy: it is experience that brings us down to the world of reality. What is it that in youth sheds a dewy light round the evening star? That makes the daisy look so bright? That perfumes the hyacinth? That embalms the first kiss of love? It is the delight of novelty, and the seeing no end to the pleasure that we fondly believe is still in store for us. The heart revels in the luxury of its own thoughts, and is unable to sustain the weight of hope and love that presses upon it...In this respect the soul comes into the world "in utter nakedness." Love waits for the ripening of the youthful blood. The sense of pleasure precedes the love of pleasure, but with the sense of pleasure, as soon as it is felt, come thronging infinite desires and hopes of pleasure, and love is mature as soon as born. It withers and it dies almost as soon!

This play presents a beautiful *coup-d'oeil* of the progress of human life. In thought it occupies years, and embraces the circle of the affections from childhood to old age. Juliet has become a great girl, a young woman since we first remember her a little thing in the idle prattle of the nurse. Lady Capulet was about her age when she became a mother, and old Capulet somewhat impatiently tells his younger visitors,

> — I've seen the day,
> That I have worn a visor, and could tell
> A whispering tale in a fair lady's ear,
> Such as would please: 'tis gone, 'tis gone, 'tis gone.

Thus one period of life makes way for the following, and one generation pushes another off the stage. One of the most striking passages to show the intense feeling of youth in this play is Capulet's invitation to Paris to visit his entertainment.

> At my poor house, look to behold this night
> Earth-treading stars that make dark heav'n light;
> Such comfort as do lusty young men feel
> When well-apparel'd April on the heel
> Of limping winter treads, even such delight
> Among fresh female-buds shall you this night
> Inherit at my house.

The feelings of youth and of the spring are here blended together like the breath of opening flowers. Images of vernal beauty appear to have floated before the author's mind, in writing this poem, in profusion. Here is another of exquisite beauty, brought in more by accident than by necessity. Montague declares of his son smit with a hopeless passion, which he will not reveal —

> But he, his own affection's counsellor,
> Is to himself so secret and so close,
> So far from sounding and discovery,
> As is the bud bit with an envious worm,
> Ere he can spread his sweet leaves to the air,
> Or dedicate his beauty to the sun.

This casual description is as full of passionate beauty as when Romeo dwells in frantic fondness on "the white wonder of his Juliet's hand." The reader may, if he pleases, contrast the exquisite pastoral simplicity of the above lines with the gorgeous description of Juliet when Romeo first sees her at her father's house, surrounded by company and artificial splendour.

> What lady's that which doth enrich the hand
> Of yonder knight?
> O she doth teach the torches to burn bright;
> Her beauty hangs upon the cheek of night,
> Like a rich jewel in an Æthiop's ear.

It would be hard to say which of the two garden scenes is the finest, that where he first converses with his love, or takes leave of her the morning after their marriage. Both are like a heaven upon earth; the

113

blissful bowers of Paradise let down upon this lower world. We will give only one passage of these well known scenes to shew the perfect refinement and delicacy of Shakespear's conception of the female character. It is wonderful how Collins, who was a critic and a poet of great sensibility, should have encouraged the common error on this subject by saying — "But stronger Shakespear felt for man alone."

The passage we mean is Juliet's apology for her maiden boldness.

> Thou know'st the mask of night is on my face;
> Else would a maiden blush bepaint my cheek
> For that which thou hast heard me speak to-night.
> Fain would I dwell on form, fain, fain deny
> What I have spoke — but farewel compliment:
> Dost thou love me? I know thou wilt say, ay,
> And I will take thee at thy word — Yet if thou swear'st,
> Thou may'st prove false; at lovers' perjuries
> They say Jove laughs. Oh gentle Romeo,
> If thou dost love, pronounce it faithfully;
> Or if thou think I am too quickly won,
> I'll frown and be perverse, and say thee nay,
> So thou wilt woo: but else not for the world.
> In truth, fair Montague, I am too fond;
> And therefore thou may'st think my 'haviour light;
> But trust me, gentleman, I'll prove more true
> Than those that have more cunning to be strange.
> I should have been more strange, I must confess
> But that thou over-heard'st, ere I was ware,
> My true love's passion; therefore pardon me,
> And not impute this yielding to light love,
> Which the dark night hath so discovered.

In this and all the rest, her heart, fluttering between pleasure, hope, and fear, seems to have dictated to her tongue, and "calls true love spoken simple modesty" ... Some critics do not perceive that the feelings of the heart sanctify, without disguising, the impulses of nature. Without refinement themselves, they confound modesty with hypocrisy. Not so the German critic, Schlegel. Speaking of *Romeo and Juliet*, he says, "It was reserved for Shakespear to unite purity of heart and the glow of imagination, sweetness and dignity of manners and passionate violence, in one ideal picture." The character is indeed one of perfect truth and sweetness. It has nothing forward, nothing coy, nothing affected or coquettish about it; — it is pure effusion of nature. It is as frank as it is modest, for it has no thought that it wishes to conceal. It reposes in conscious innocence on the strength of its affections. Its delicacy does not consist in coldness and reserve, but in combining warmth of imagination and tenderness of heart with the most voluptuous sensibility. Love is a gentle flame that rarifies and expands her whole being. What an idea of trembling haste and airy grace, borne upon the thoughts of love, does the Friar's exclamation give of her, as she approaches his cell to be married —

> Here comes the lady. Oh, so light of foot
> Will ne'er wear out the everlasting flint:
> A lover may bestride the gossamer,
> That idles in the wanton summer air,
> And yet not fall, so light is vanity.

The tragic part of this character is of a piece with the rest. It is the heroic founded on tenderness and delicacy. Of this kind are her resolution to follow the Friar's advice, and the conflict in her bosom between apprehension and love when she comes to take the sleeping poison. Shakespear is blamed for the mixture of low characters. If this is a deformity, it is the source of a thousand beauties. One instance is the contrast between the guileless simplicity of Juliet's attachment to her first love, and the convenient policy of the nurse in advising her to marry Paris, which excites such indignation in her mistress. "Ancient damnation! oh most wicked fiend," etc.

Romeo is Hamlet in love. There is the same rich exuberance of passion and sentiment in the one, that there is of thought and sentiment in the other. Both are absent and self-involved, both live out of themselves in a world of imagination. Hamlet is abstracted from every thing; Romeo is abstracted from every thing but his love, and lost in it. His "frail thoughts dally with faint surmise," and are fashioned out of the suggestions of hope, "the flatteries of sleep." He is himself only in his Juliet; she is his only reality, his heart's true home and idol. The rest of the world is to him a passing dream. How finely is this character portrayed where he recollects himself on seeing Paris slain at the tomb of Juliet! —

> What said my man, when my betossed soul
> Did not attend him as we rode? I think
> He told me Paris should have married Juliet.

...Romeo's passion for Juliet is not a first love: it succeeds and drives out his passion for another mistress, Rosaline, as the sun hides the stars. This is perhaps an artifice (not absolutely necessary) to give us a higher opinion of the lady, while the first absolute surrender of her heart to him enhances the richness of the prize. The commencement, progress, and ending of his second passion are however complete in themselves, not injured if they are not bettered by the first. The outline of the play is taken from an Italian novel; but the dramatic arrangement of the different scenes between the lovers, the more than dramatic interest in the progress of the story, the developement of the characters with time and circumstances, just according to the degree and kind of interest excited, are not inferior to the expression of passion and nature. It has been ingeniously remarked among other proofs of skill in the contrivance of the fable, that the improbability of the main incident in the piece, the administering of the sleeping-potion, is softened and obviated from the beginning by the introduction of the Friar on his first appearance culling simples and descanting on their virtues. Of the passionate scenes in this tragedy, that between the Friar and Romeo when he is told of his sentence of banishment, that between Juliet and the Nurse when she hears of it, and of the death of her cousin Tybalt (which bears no proportion in her mind, when passion after the first shock of surprise throws its weight into the scale of her affections) and the last scene at the tomb, are among the most natural and overpowering. In all of these it is not merely the force of any one passion that is given, but the slightest and most unlooked-for transitions from one to another, the mingling currents of every different feeling rising up and prevailing in turn, swayed by the master-mind of the poet, as the waves undulate beneath the gliding storm . . .

William Hazlitt

For a sight of him [Shakespeare], authentically himself, but still adolescent in his art, experimenting impulsively with couplet, quatrain, blank verse, prose, passing from convention to spontaneity and back to convention, for a very epitome of this first stage of his development look into *Romeo and Juliet*. The verse at the beginning is smooth and swift; too smooth and swift to cut out character as it flows. The music of it is descriptive; in tune as well as words the Prince's speech is stern authority incarnate, yet he himself is nobody. Montague and Benvolio paint for us the lovesick Romeo more vividly than they paint themselves. Romeo takes up the painting; and here is youthful character so far realised that we have him self-consciously picturing himself as he wishes to be seen. But we are also conscious of the dramatist at work, and of his verse and its charm. Then, in the third scene:

Enter Lady Capulet and Nurse.

Lady C. Nurse, where's my daughter? Call her forth to me.

Nurse.   Now, by my maidenhead at twelve year old,
            I bade her come. What, lamb! What, ladybird!
            God forbid! Where's this girl? What, Juliet! . . .

— and suddenly (who, watching the play, has not felt it?) the barriers of artifice drop, and beside *this* reality, the very stage and the solid theatre become unreal. We do not note for the moment whether it is rhyme, blank verse or prose that is being spoken; vivid character has made the whole dramatic medium incandescent.

These speeches of the Nurse are Shakespeare's first unequivocal triumph in the molding of the blank verse convention to the seemingly spontaneous expression of character. Analyse them; every accent, every pause and fresh impulse to the rhythm has its revealing purpose. Yet he seems to be working in perfect freedom. Yet, again, he keeps all the compelling power which the music of verse can give him.

With *Romeo and Juliet*, we find Shakespeare definitely set towards his end — which is, indeed, the end of all drama — the projection of character in action. And his advance will be to an ever deeper, richer, subtler conception and expression of character; finally also, to reflection in a man's expression of himself of the world in which he spiritually dwells. That last step, however, is still far ahead with the great tragedies. He is searching now for appropriate form; never content to take this ready-made. Turn to Mercutio and mark the change from the verse of the "Queen Mab" speech — charming, but expressive of anybody and nobody — to the prose of the death scene; the man is himself by then. Mark the development in the expression of Romeo with the development of his character; from the self-conscious lover making conventional complaint, through the pure emotion of the love-making and the passion bred from Mercutio's death and Tybalt's, to the achievement of tragic simplicity in his answer to the fatal news:

> Is it even so? Then I defy you, stars!

its acceptance with

> Well, Juliet, I will lie with thee to-night.

He turns convention to dramatic account when he enshrines the first meeting of the lovers in a sonnet; it gives him the very touch of delicate shy formality that he needs. The method of the "balcony" scene is apt. It abounds in conventional imagery, made fresh again by the music of the setting . . .

Part of the effect is gained by the resolution from picturesque phrase to commonplace. Beauty of words can add nothing to their love, and its beauty makes the simplest — the silliest! — things beautiful. Shakespeare clarifies his medium here to entire transparency; yet (again) none of the value of the medium itself is lost. Anyone, surely, could write as simply! Perhaps. But to wed simplicity to poetic and dramatic power, that is another matter.

We may find less to praise in the spasmodic return to convention — to the extreme of artifice, indeed — when, a few scenes later, Juliet has to meet the news of Tybalt's death. This, for distraction and rage:

> O serpent heart, hid with a flowering face!
> Did ever dragon keep so fair a cave?
> Beautiful tyrant, fiend angelical!
> Dove feathered raven! wolfish ravening lamb! . . .

might have been lifted entire from *Henry VI*. And the cascade of puns upon "I", "ay" and "eye" which follows (and which no acve been lifted entirely from *Henry VI*. And the cascade of puns upon "I", "ay" and "eye" which follows (and which no actress of Juliet is nowadays asked to face) may seem, for the moment, to destroy the dramatic illusion altogether.

It will not have done so for Elizabethan audiences. Shakespeare, it is true, soon and finally abandoned such polyonymous apostrophes. He never abandoned the pun itself, though he grew thrifty in his use of it. But the pun was not then necessarily comic. We may think of the

Elizabethans as so in love wish their language and its new-found strength that even play with it delighted them and did not seem ridiculous. In

> Now is it Rome indeed and room enough
> When there is in it but one only man,

and in

> I'll gild the faces of the grooms withal
> For it must seem their guilt.

there was the stimulus of surprise, and an added power of emphasis, to which we no longer so readily respond...

For the apparent retrogression from spontaneity to verbal convention of whatever kind (and Shakespeare does this with Romeo too; also, notably, in the concerted scene of the mourning over Juliet's supposed dead body) we shall see the excuse if we remember that he is not composing and perfecting a poem, but preparing a play to be acted; and that, besides, he may well be in something of a hurry. He has to tell his story dramatically and provide his actors with the means of making certain effects. No difficulty if the characters are alive in his mind and will rise to each occasion, spontaneously expressive! But suppose one of them suddenly will not. You cannot shirk the occasion and its effect; your play requires just this.At this precise moment you need a Juliet in a passion, a Romeo in despair, or a chourus of grief. So if passion, despair or grief will not spring spontaneously and expressively, you fall back upon a convention, a formula. And you do so because it is a thing the actor understands, and *you can trust him to do the rest*. You have at least provided him with material for the effect.

Harley Granville-Barker

...I should like to take a poetic tragedy — *Romeo and Juliet* — and examine its use of dramatic imagery in a few key scenes. Granted the possibility of a criticism both holistic and dramatic, what does it tell us of the imagery of the play? I believe that it can tell us a great deal, but that what it yields is in the first instance disappointing. We had hoped that it was a greater play than it seems to be — an adolescent hope, perhaps; and we wonder where the fault lies — in our method or in the play. On closer examination, we worry less; for there are certain things we should keep in mind. One is that the play is an early work, that it is in some ways more artful than artistic. We should not expect the mastery of an older and wiser Shakespeare. We should beware of the danger of reading the play in the great shadow of *Hamlet* and *King Lear*, and we should endeavor to see it in the context which it creates for itself.

Another factor to be remembered concerns our method — that of a holistic criticism. For all its virtues, let us not forget that it is a method which will go to enormous lengths to seek out a complexity, whether real or imagined. And *Romeo and Juliet* is not a particularly complex play; it obviously lacks the weight and magnitude of the great tragedies. Yet even here a holistic criticism can be of use. Because *Romeo and Juliet* is not so profound as the more massive tragedies, and because its use of imagery is now dramatic, now merely poetic, analysis should prove all the more valuable in showing wherein differences lie. For such a purpose, *Romeo and Juliet* tells us perhaps more than a greater play would do. I think we shall find that what seems merely decorative and undramatic at first inspection will often prove to have a far closer relation to the play's essential integrity than we might have expected. *Romeo and Juliet* is its own world, and it is a curious world in which the decorative is often made essential, as in the best baroque architecture.

The play opens with the entrance of Sampson and Gregory, two cowardly servants of the House of Capulet. Their purpose, at least in part, is to set the quarrelsome background to the tragedy which is to come. They anticipate struggles far greater than their own, and the bawdy of their speech is not without relevance. They pun on "maiden heads," on "sense," perhaps even on the words "tool" and "naked weapon." I should not wish to push the matter too far, yet in this punning and in the rather base imagery of the servants' speech there is a thematic relation to the developing play. *Romeo and Juliet*, for all its beauty, is not one of the great documents of the human spirit. It is a play in which erotic love comes to grief; and the low talk of Sampson and Gregory is not without relation to the intense eroticism of the young lovers themselves. The images which the servants use in the play's opening lines have their own dramatic point and effectiveness. They inform us of the feud upon which the tragedy hinges; but, through the medium of the pun, they also anticipate the great and sensual love of the protagonists.

Scarcely seventy-odd lines of the play have been spoken when Benvolio and Tybalt are fighting furiously in the street. The citizens of Verona and, later, Prince Escalus enter to put a stop to the swordplay. The Prince's speech is interesting, as it presents an instance of a very simple, even obvious use of dramatic imagery. But the simplicity of the images takes dignity from a device of another kind — from a formality of phrase and cadence which recalls the royal speeches of the history plays. Imagery is but one of the many modes of expression to which the poetic dramatist has access:

> Three civil brawls, bred of an airy word,
> By thee, old Capulet and Montague,
> Have thrice disturb'd the quiet of our streets
> And made Verona's ancient citizens
> Cast by their grave beseeming ornaments
> To wield old partisans, in hands as old,
> Canker'd with peace, to part your canker'd hate.

Here is an obvious reference to the insult which the State suffers at the hands of discordant and rebellious subjects. Even more important is the reiterated play upon the word "old," along with other references to

119

age. There is a certain visual and contextual pertinence in such imagery. For one thing, the old people, the elder Montagues and Capulets, are present on the stage as the Prince speaks, as are the citizenry with "old partisans, in hands as old." Now all this serves to underscore certain truths: that these people are too old to be quarrelling, that even their quarrel itself is old, and that peace, not contention, should be the occupation of old age. It is no wonder, then, that their bluster is all out of proportion to the "airy word" that gave it birth. And the references to "canker'd," and through this adjectival form back to the noun, "canker," the disease of old age, give further emphasis to the idea of maturity gone far astray. This in turn relates to the theme of the play, which may be seen from one point of view as the dramatic conflict between youth and youth's elders. In other words, we have here a very simple and reasonably effective use of dramatic imagery. It relates both to the visual composition upon the stage and to the comprehensive thematic unity of the play. It possesses, finally, a certain economy of means.

...Benvolio's speech to Romeo's mother introduces the light-darkness antithesis which is to dominate so much of the action. Similar imagery occurs in the balcony scene, in other of the love scenes and soliloquies about love, and in the scene at the Capulet family tomb with which the play ends. By that time, the light-dark imagery has become so complex, perhaps even so ambiguous, that it both dominates and undermines the play's essential statement. What do light and dark mean in the special world of *Romeo and Juliet*? To begin with, we may take them as the simplest of Jungian archetypes: Light is a good thing, and dark is a bad one. Light provides warmth and protection from one's enemies; dark offers no warmth and no protection.

But *Romeo and Juliet* is in most essentials a Christian play; it is manifestly the product of a Christian culture. We would do well, then, to remember the *Lux in tenebris lucet* of Saint John, where the Light is that of Christ, or at least of Christian Truth, and the Darkness that of Sin. Now we may be very loth to see Romeo and Juliet as sinners; at the very worst our modern secularism can view them as guilty only of error. But even this lends an added dimension to the play. Error is more than accident; it is at least human and not impersonal; and it allows some sort of tragic view, which accident does not.

Against all this may be urged the emphasis on the "star-cross'd lovers" and Friar Laurence's letter undelivered in Mantua; and such an emphasis must be granted, along with the manifestly arbitrary course of the action itself. What I would wish to call attention to, however, is that the setting and imagery, especially much of the light imagery, would often seem to indicate a more tragic and meaningful play than would the action as an abstract from the whole. This unresolved ambiguity is, I think, a fault and not a virtue.

Benvolio's speech to Madame Montague, wherein he describes her

120

son's love-sick state, opens with a reference to the sun . . .

It is beautiful poetry; it comes to an actor's tongue with easy grace, but note also that it introduces imagery of great dramatic effectiveness. Here are images which relate, which belong to the play as something intrinsic and indispensable. Here a theme is introduced; and as the play progresses these early references to light and dark take on an added significance, especially if we see in them a broad and perhaps specifically Christian symbolism. These initial references contribute to more than theme alone; they introduce Romeo and are the beginning of his characterization. They are, moreover, suitable to him who speaks and to her who is spoken to. Benvolio is also sick at heart; and in this he bears a likeness to Romeo, while the elegance of his speech befits the age and character of the woman he addresses.

In the speech which follows, that of old Montague, Romeo's characterization and the play's thematic emphasis gather interest. Particularly important is the description of the young man's conduct at dawn:

> Away from light steals home my heavy son,
> And private in his chamber pens himself,
> Shuts up his windows, locks fair daylight out,
> And makes himself an artificial night.

The words upon which I should like to lay greatest stress are in the line about "artificial night," for in a sense this play is a study of the artificial, perhaps most so when we least expect it. It is not only about young love, but about Love, which is not precisely the same thing. It is about the sense of sight, about appearance and reality; and the imagery bears this out. The sense most frequently resorted to is that of sight. Now this is common enough in poetry of all kinds, indeed, almost inevitable. Though I can offer no statistical proof, I am persuaded that we have more words relating to seeing than to touch, smell, hearing, or taste. I would even suggest that *Romeo and Juliet* goes beyond the high proportion of sight images usual in English poetry.

And there is artificiality, too. It is not enough to dismiss this as the verbal trickery of a young dramatist, as a condition necessary to his fledgling art. Artificiality belongs to the tragedy, is a part of it; it permeates much of the imagery; it fits the characters and the situation in which they find themselves. Nor will it do to limit this to the Romeo of the play's opening, to say merely that there he is in love with love, that later he loves more profoundly. True, he does; but there is a self-conscious emotional posturing in the "pilgrim" sonnet he and Juliet speak to each other at their meeting, even as there is an element of artificiality in the balcony scene.

Manners are most useful in crisis. Pose belongs to their situation and is perhaps nowhere better seen than in their love of paradox, especially at points of great dramatic stress. That imagery which at times seems most strained is often quite just and appropriate. Such imagery relates dramatically to the situation in which it occurs. Whatever failure of

121

tragic range there may be usually lies in the situation and action, not in the imagery. We wear the habit of Christian symbolism — *en habillements bourgeois*; and *Romeo and Juliet* persists in metaphors drawn from the Christian symbolism of light and dark. The doctrinal weight of such images is often too great for the story, and this disparity between symbolic function and the fable in which it is embodied can perhaps best be explained as a part of the Renaissance alteration of medieval Christian values.

Whatever its exact habitual content, Jungian or Christian, the light-dark antithesis is set up early in the play; and we are not surprised at the verbal exchange between Benvolio and Romeo, upon Romeo's first entrance:

> *Ben.*   Good morrow, cousin.
> *Romeo.*   Is the day so young?
> *Ben.*   But new struck nine.
> *Romeo.*   Ay me, sad hours seem long . . .

This relates beautifully to what has gone before and stands in fine ironic contrast to the haste which is to characterize the sequent action. The speeches of Romeo which follow, being a sort of long and paradoxical moan, are in keeping with what we have just learned of his character. The same is true of this exchange between the two friends, in which the theme of sight, or that of appearance and reality, is touched upon:

> *Romeo.*   O teach me how I should forget to think.
> *Ben.*   By giving liberty unto thine eyes;
> Examine other beauties . . .

And, four lines later:

> *Romeo.*   He that is strucken blind cannot forget
> The precious treasure of his eyesight lost:
> Show me a mistress that is passing fair,
> What doth her beauty serve but as a note
> Where I may read who pass'd that passing fair?

There is in the play's imagery much emphasis upon reading, books, and generally scholarly paraphernalia; this is, I think, a further instance of a more general insistence upon sight and the possible failure of sight, or in a wider sense, upon judgment and lack of judgment in a world where morality informs imagery and deforms action . . .

Randolf M. Bulgin

Bibliography

Bradby, Anne, ed., *Shakespeare Criticism 1919-1935*. New York, Oxford University Press, 1936.

Bradley, A.C., *Shakespearean Tragedy*. New York, Macmillan, 1904.

Clemen, Wolfgang, *The Development of Shakespeare's Imagery*. Cambridge, Harvard University Press, 1951.

Charlton, H.B., *Shakespearian Tragedy*. New York, Cambridge University Press, 1930

Dean, Leonard, ed., *Shakespeare: Modern Essays in Criticism*. New York, Oxford University Press, 1957.

De Rougemont, Denis, *Love in the Western World*. New York, Doubleday & Co., 1959

Harbage, Alfred, *As They Liked It: an Essay on Shakespeare and Morality*. New York, Macmillan Co., 1947.

————— ed., *Shakespeare's Tragedies*. Englewood, Spectrum Series, Prentice-Hall, 1964.

Moore, Olin H., *The Legend of Romeo and Juliet*. Columbus, Ohio State University Press, 1950

Moulton, Richard G., *Shakespeare as a Dramatic Artist*. New York, Oxford University Press, 1929.

Partridge, Eric, *Shakespeare's Bawdy*. New York, E.P. Dutton, 1960.

Seward, James H., *Tragic Vision in Romeo and Juliet*. Wilmington, N.C., Consortium, 1973.

Spurgeon, Caroline, *Shakespeare's Imagery and What It Tells Us*. New York, Cambridge University Press, 1935.

Stauffer, Donald, *Shakespeare's World of Images*. New York, W.W. Norton & Co., 1949.

Stoll, Elmer E., *Shakespeare's Young Lovers*. New York, Oxford University Press, 1937.

Traversi, D.A., *An Approach to Shakespeare*. New York, Doubleday Anchor, 1956.

Van Doren, Mark, *Shakespeare*. New York, Henry Holt & Co., 1939.

Williams, George W., *The Most Excellent and Lamentable Tragedie of Romeo and Juliet*. Durham, North Carolina, Duke University Press, 1964.

only when you need to knock
on wood,

Do you realize that the
world is made up entirly
of e lumnium & plastic

Journal Topic   discribe a situation
                 where you have

dramatic irony pg.37

        overjoyed

              Something